Also by Solomon Volkov

Testimony: The Memoirs of Dmitri Shostakovich

Balanc

Tch

TRANSLATED FROM THE RUSSIAN BY

ANTONINA W. BOUIS

ine's

INTERVIEWS WITH GEORGE BALANCHINE

BY SOLOMON VOLKOV

aikovsky

SIMON AND SCHUSTER · NEW YORK

Published by Simon and Schuster
A Division of Simon & Schuster, Inc.
Simon & Schuster Building
Rockefeller Center
1230 Avenue of the Americas
New York, New York 10020
SIMON AND SCHUSTER and colophon
are registered trademarks of Simon & Schuster, Inc.
Designed by Edith Fowler
Production directed by Richard L. Willett
Manufactured in the United States of America

10   9   8   7   6   5   4   3   2   1

Library of Congress Cataloging in Publication Data

Volkov, Solomon.
  Balanchine's Tchaikovsky.

  Includes index.
   1. Tchaikovsky, Peter Ilich, 1840–1893.
2. Ballet.   3. Balanchine, George.   4. Choreographers—
United States—Interviews.   I. Balanchine, George.
II. Title.
ML410.C4V583   1985   780'.92'4   84-26716
ISBN: 0-671-49875-4

Simon & Schuster gratefully acknowledges the kind permission
of the Estate of George Balanchine.

Page 4: photograph of George Balanchine by Carolyn George.
Page 5: portrait of Tchaikovsky by Nikolai Kuznetsov, 1893.

CONTENTS

	Preface	11
	Introduction: *George Balanchine, in Interview*	27
ONE	*Tchaikovsky and Balanchine*	31
TWO	*Childhood*	39
THREE	*St. Petersburg*	51
FOUR	*The Man*	73
FIVE	*Reading and Travel*	95
SIX	*Predecessors and Contemporaries*	109
SEVEN	*"But the Music Is So Noble!"*	117
EIGHT	*Operas*	133
NINE	Swan Lake *and* The Sleeping Beauty	143
TEN	The Nutcracker	175
ELEVEN	*Craftsmen*	195
TWELVE	*Stravinsky*	203
THIRTEEN	*"Russian Roulette"*	219
	Chronologies	227
	Index	245

PREFACE

On February 14, 1981, I had an extraordinary chance meeting with the choreographer George Balanchine. It happened on Broadway, not far from Lincoln Center, next to a small shop called the Nevada Meat Market. I recognized Balanchine's face and characteristic gait, and acting on impulse I decided to approach him, even though we were not acquainted. I greeted him in Russian ("*Dobryi den', Georgy Melitonovich!*") and introduced myself. Balanchine, apparently agreeable to being accosted in the middle of New York by some Russian émigré he didn't know, stopped and struck up a conversation with me. The newspapers had just reported that his company, the New York City Ballet, was planning a Tchaikovsky festival. We started to talk about Tchaikovsky.

Rather, Balanchine talked. I responded occasionally. What I heard astonished me. Here I was, a thirty-six-year-old musicologist from the Soviet Union, thinking that I knew all about Tchaikovsky; yet this relaxed, gray-haired man, who

12   had left Russia fifty-seven years ago at the age of twenty, was discussing Tchaikovsky from a viewpoint rarely explored in the Soviet Union. He talked about Tchaikovsky as a great craftsman, a genius "goldsmith" who worked on his compositions with diligence and care, while achieving an impression of artistic abandon and spontaneity.*

I was awed by Balanchine's brilliant and paradoxical argument. At the same time, my own few remarks must have made sense to Balanchine, because he abruptly broke off his lecture and suggested, "Write about it." "What?" "Write about Tchaikovsky's craftsmanship," he explained. "For our festival booklet." He bade me good-bye and went into the meat market. I was left dumbfounded. I didn't know then that Balanchine often made decisions out of casual chats on the street.

As soon as I was home I wrote down every detail of Balanchine's conversation. Then, trying to be as succinct as possible, I wrote a short essay on Tchaikovsky in Russian, based on Balanchine's ideas, and sent it to him. Evidently it met with Balanchine's approval, for it appeared in English translation in the souvenir brochure of the New York City Ballet Tchaikovsky Festival.

One reason why this was so remarkable an experience for me was that while I loved Tchaikovsky deeply and *felt* the composer's majesty, Balanchine *understood* why Tchaikovsky was so great and took pains to explain and clarify it for me, a professional musicologist.

Before the Tchaikovsky festival began, I met with Balanchine several more times for further conversations about Tchaikovsky; I tape-recorded some of them with Balanchine's

---

* In fact, this was an unusual treatment of Tchaikovsky even by Western standards. It is only recently that articles like Henry Zajaczkowsky's "The Function of Obsessive Elements in Tchaikovsky's Style" (*The Music Review*, February 1982), have begun to appear in Western musicological publications.

permission and took shorthand notes of others. Sitting on a wooden chair in his office at Lincoln Center's State Theater—a chair recommended by his doctor for his back, he said—Balanchine led me on a dazzling trip into the past.

14   A strikingly new, and in many respects controversial, image of Tchaikovsky emerged for me, quite at odds with both the "great humanist and progressive artist" of Soviet textbooks and sentimental, near maniacal melancholic of Western pop biographies. I heard a genius speaking about a genius. Balanchine had been involved in Tchaikovsky's music throughout his artistic life. He had choreographed at least a dozen important ballets to Tchaikovsky's compositions. Balanchine's knowledge of Tchaikovsky's works was second to none. Even more remarkably, I sensed a deep personal involvement. I could see that Tchaikovsky was still alive for Balanchine, that he actually felt himself to be in continual communication with the composer. There was a compelling urgency in Balanchine's outpourings.

Balanchine's portrait of Tchaikovsky was highly subjective, yet nonetheless vivid and convincing. This was Balanchine's Tchaikovsky—a St. Petersburger to the marrow of his bones; a sophisticated "European from Russia" *au courant* in Western culture, but at the same time a true Russian patriot and staunch monarchist, and, naturally, as deeply devout as Balanchine himself.

Balanchine was drawn to Tchaikovsky the craftsman, an artist who meticulously built up the stage and musical effects in his works, who was ready to fulfill any commission and was not ashamed to call some of his compositions "my wares." Balanchine spoke animatedly about Tchaikovsky the innovator, who enriched the musical vocabulary with bold new harmonies and exquisite orchestral colors. And, understandably, he never tired of praising Tchaikovsky's incomparable ballet music for having overturned all the old canons and for having played a liberating, even revolutionary, role for composers and choreographers to come. Gradually, I came to understand the seemingly paradoxical statement Balanchine made upon

announcing the City Ballet's Tchaikovsky festival: "I don't believe Tchaikovsky is Romantic, I believe he's modern."

At the same time, Balanchine was quick to recall the influential cultural traditions of Russia's past, invoking the
names of the revered greats of Tchaikovsky's personal pan-
theon—the poet Alexander Pushkin and the composer Mikhail Glinka. Here Balanchine was true to an important
modernist principle. As George Steiner remarked in his *After
Babel* (1975): "We know now that the modernist movement
which dominated art, music, letters during the first half of the
century was, at critical points, a strategy of conservation, of
custodianship. Stravinsky's genius developed through phases
of recapitulation."

Of course, this Tchaikovsky very much resembled Balanchine himself. It became clearer and clearer to me that Balanchine identified with Tchaikovsky, that when he spoke of
Tchaikovsky he was also speaking of himself. For Balanchine,
a circumspect and intensely private person, this was a way—
typically Petersburgian, incidentally—to reveal some of his
most-guarded thoughts, opinions, and even self-doubts. Balanchine defined his own aesthetic and moral judgments by
comparing them to Tchaikovsky's. His portrait of Tchaikovsky was simultaneously an attempt, perhaps unconscious,
at a self-portrait.

I felt myself compelled to preserve this unique double
portrait and bring it to the public in Balanchine's own words.
It was my obligation—more, my duty: as a fellow Russian
émigré, as an alumnus of the conservatory attended by both
Tchaikovsky and Balanchine, and as an ardent admirer of the
art of both men.

So I wrote a letter to Balanchine proposing to do a children's book about Tchaikovsky—something simple and unpretentious. Admittedly this was a ploy to engage Balanchine's

18 interest. By then I was well aware of his dislike of elaborate, "meaningful" statements, of pompous eloquence. I also knew of his special feeling for childhood and children, a feeling shared by so many people who become professional musicians, dancers, or athletes early in life, moving abruptly from childhood to adulthood.

Tchaikovsky would be the "coauthor" of the book, I suggested to Balanchine. He would be represented by his own writings. Balanchine would comment on selections I would prepare from the composer's letters and diaries, and I would record those comments, then organize and shape them. I argued that there was a real need for such a book. A strange situation exists, I emphasized: people love to listen to Tchaikovsky's music, but many seem to be ashamed to show their respect and admiration for the composer the way aficionados of Mozart, Beethoven, or Brahms do. Balanchine had to help Tchaikovsky's secret admirers come out into the open. Balanchine's commentaries on Tchaikovsky the Petersburger would be unique not only because of his close involvement with Tchaikovsky's "imperial" music, but also because, I wrote quite bluntly, Balanchine was one of the last living Petersburgers, an endangered species. The heritage of St. Petersburg, destroyed by the hurricanes of history, was buried underwater, like Atlantis, and soon there would be no one to remember it and tell about it. So the proposed book would serve a double purpose: as a quintessential guide to Tchaikovsky, and as an important source for understanding the great Russian culture of a bygone era.

After I brought the letter to Balanchine by hand, explaining that I would be too embarrassed to speak to him on the subject face-to-face, I went off and waited anxiously. Finally, Barbara Horgan, Balanchine's personal assistant, called and informed me, "He thinks it's a good idea."

Meanwhile, an episode occurred that may have helped

OVERLEAF: *Solomon Volkov and George Balanchine*

me in this delicate cause. After the premiere of the new version of Balanchine's ballet *Mozartiana*, set to Tchaikovsky's orchestral suite, I sent him a short note, as usual in Russian. Then one day Barbara Horgan asked me for an English translation of the letter. I obliged without asking why it was needed. Only later and quite by chance did I learn that Balanchine had ordered my letter inserted as a program note to his *Mozartiana*. This, I was told, produced something of a commotion in the small, closed world of the New York ballet, mainly because, as Arlene Croce commented in *The New Yorker* in seeming disbelief, "It is unlike Balanchine to use a fan letter to plug one of his ballets."

Yes, it was quite unlike Balanchine; so why did he do it? I quote my letter: "Your interpretation revealed the inner sadness and delicate harmony of this music. How subtly sketched in *Gigue* the flourishing bow of the Russian composer to the Austrian genius! The dance does not follow the music, mirroring its meter and rhythm. It draws the music into a complex counterpoint. . . ." For Arlene Croce, the key word in the letter appeared to be "counterpoint"; a counterpoint between music and dance in Balanchine's ballet. For me, the key word was "bow": in his *Mozartiana* suite, Tchaikovsky paid homage to his god Mozart; by the same token, in the ballet *Mozartiana*, Balanchine paid homage to Tchaikovsky, to the Russian composer's ties with European culture, and to his St. Petersburg mastery of stylization.

The proposed book about Tchaikovsky I was suggesting would be in the same manner, only this time Balanchine would express his homage in words rather than dance movements. Apparently, Balanchine was ready to embark on the project. Despite his acknowledged skepticism at the ability of words to explain music, he wanted to preserve through the power of the printed word at least some of his knowledge and intuitive understanding of Tchaikovsky.

20   And so we began to work. I would bring along to our meetings (which usually took place backstage at the State Theater) index cards on which I had typed quotations from Tchaikovsky's letters and diaries and also from reminiscences of the composer's friends. Balanchine would then comment on the quotes in that inimitably spontaneous and paradoxical manner of his. As before, I tape-recorded some of our conversations and took shorthand notes of others. Balanchine's Russian was flawless, with the old Petersburg pronunciation, but he sprinkled his speech with words and idioms from French, German, and English. It was delightful to listen to him.

During 1981 and 1982, Balanchine and I had thirty-three conversations on Tchaikovsky. The meetings did not always go smoothly. Anyone who knew Balanchine would hardly have expected them to. Sometimes he was in no mood to talk. Often he thought my questions stupid and got angry. Then again, he would become exaggeratedly courteous and complimentary: "You know all that better than I." As a rule this did not bode well; he would close himself off more than he did on the angry occasions.

In these difficulties of working with him, Balanchine reminded me of the composer Dmitri Shostakovich, also a Petersburger, on whose memoirs I collaborated in the early seventies, when I was still living in Russia. Both Shostakovich and Balanchine were unpredictable. Both could be peevish and arbitrary, though neither ever raised his voice. Both occasionally behaved like children. And those were the best moments. But Balanchine was a much more elegant child, given his upbringing at St. Petersburg's Maryinsky ballet school.

As he spoke, majestic imperial St. Petersburg came to life. Even though I had lived for fourteen years in that city (which by then was, of course, called Leningrad), and even though I had personally known some of the people Balanchine was talking about, such as the poet Anna Akhmatova and the choreographer Fyodor Lopukhov, Balanchine's Petersburg still appeared to me like a newly magical and mysterious place, a realm where anything—but anything—could happen.

Several times we discussed the controversial question of Tchaikovsky's untimely death in St. Petersburg. Balanchine was certain that it had been suicide. For him the composer's tragic end was an important part of the Tchaikovsky legend. Modernism leaned heavily on the Romantic myth of the persecuted artist, condemned to death by a Philistine society, and I saw that Balanchine was deeply troubled by this theme. His obsession with it was reflected not only in his ballet *Davidsbündlertänze* to Schumann but also in the strange and unforgettable *Adagio Lamentoso*, a profoundly personal tribute to Tchaikovsky, staged by Balanchine to the composer's Sixth Symphony, the *Pathétique*.

I challenged Balanchine, pointing out that Tchaikovsky was, after all, a religious man, for whom suicide would constitute a mortal sin. In response, Balanchine startled me by suggesting the idea of "Russian roulette." I had never heard anything like it in the disputes about Tchaikovsky's death. It came as a new and quite convincing twist. In any case, in this book I present Balanchine's argument just as it was given to me. The same is true of other instances in which Balanchine's views may seem controversial or unusual. I did not second-guess or gloss any of his statements.

Balanchine told me some startling things as well about Diaghilev, an early and fierce champion of Tchaikovsky. Despite the major work he did for Diaghilev, Balanchine now seemed bent on debunking the myth of the glamorous Diaghilev era. Recalling his Diaghilev years, Balanchine stressed the poverty and low social status of the Ballet Russe dancers, including himself. He vividly described humiliating confrontations with such imposing figures as Rachmaninoff and Prokofiev.

22   Without doubt, Diaghilev had enormous influence on the young choreographer, but it was Igor Stravinsky who emerged during our conversations as Balanchine's true mentor and hero. It was apparent that Balanchine considered his relationship with Stravinsky to be of the same historical importance as that between the legendary ballet master Marius Petipa and Tchaikovsky himself.

For Balanchine, Tchaikovsky and Stravinsky—one the greatest composer of ballet music of the nineteenth century, the other of the twentieth—were twin symbols of artistic greatness, and Balanchine delighted in finding parallels in their lives and work. And so it happened naturally that Stravinsky, for whom Tchaikovsky always served as an example of a "European from Russia," a cosmopolitan composer, became the third *persona dramatis* of this book. (When Balanchine decided to present a Stravinsky festival in June 1982, he asked me to write about the ties between Stravinsky and Tchaikovsky. That essay, also based on our discussions, appeared in the New York City Ballet Stravinsky Festival brochure.)

In the fall of 1982, after complications from cataract surgery, Balanchine entered New York's Roosevelt Hospital. We carried on our conversations there: I continued to bring my index cards along and to ask a lot of questions. Thus, we covered practically the entire brief and dramatic life of Tchaikovsky, from childhood to tragic death. The material gathered was, of course, not the stuff of a children's book, as we both understood, but the notion of children as a possible audience still acted as a tuning fork for us.

Balanchine was in a hurry. He kept repeating, "I still have lots to say about Tchaikovsky! We must talk!" Once he said half-jokingly, "Maybe it's a good thing that I was hospitalized. Otherwise I wouldn't have found the time to tell you all I knew." It sounded rather sad and bitter to me.

Did Balanchine in fact tell me everything he knew and

thought about Tchaikovsky? I don't think so. Gradually his
health deteriorated, and on April 30, 1983, Balanchine died at
the hospital. Obituaries the world over hailed him as one of
the greatest choreographers of all time and an artist of equal
rank to Picasso and Stravinsky.

Some time later I began to transcribe my Balanchine
tapes. It was a painful experience. Balanchine's voice came
through as if he were alive. I tried, as I began to write and organize this book, to preserve the characteristics of Balanchine's conversational style. Sometimes, for the sake of
continuity and clarity, it was necessary to combine different
segments from our discussions into a single passage. My own
conversational questions and remarks to Balanchine are omit-
ted, since they do not bear on the substance of his responses,
and it is, after all, he, not I, whose opinions are the true subject
matter of this book. The material I presented to Balanchine—
including quotes from Tchaikovsky's letters and diaries—appears in italics. Balanchine's responses and comments are in
roman type.

Would Balanchine, if he were to go through the manuscript of this book, leave everything as it is? I suppose he
would likely suggest adding some things and deleting others,
to change this and that, and perhaps to rephrase some passages. Nevertheless, this book represents, to the best of my
opinion and editorial ability, both the letter and spirit of Balanchine's thinking on Tchaikovsky.

The book would not have been possible without the involvement and encouragement of Balanchine's personal assistant, Barbara Horgan. To her I owe my deepest gratitude.

—SOLOMON VOLKOV

PUBLISHER'S NOTE

All passages in the words of George Balanchine are set in standard roman type; interlocuting passages in the words of Solomon Volkov are distinguished by italics.

INTRODUCTION

George Balanchine, in Interview

I DON'T LIKE describing things in words. I prefer to show them if possible. I demonstrate for my dancers, and they understand me. Of course, from time to time I get off a *bon mot*, something that I myself might like. But if I have to continue from there, I feel uneasy. I don't know how to do it. I'd rather answer questions.

I don't like talking about myself or the ballet. But Tchaikovsky is something else again: I know things about him that no one else does. I'm often asked about him; people are always saying, "How did that happen? What does this mean? Why is it like this?" I can't explain to everyone who asks. And I regret that sometimes. I would like to set down what I know about Tchaikovsky.

Of course, the best way to learn about Tchaikovsky is to listen to his music. But that is not as simple as it seems. In order to understand music, you have to know at least a little 27

28 about it. And to know about it, you must first try to learn to understand it.

Many books are written about Tchaikovsky, but they are not widely read. Perhaps that is because they are not very interesting. The authors display their erudition, and they search for Tchaikovsky's borrowings. "This music resembles Schumann! And what does this sound like? Aha, here's where this melody comes from!" Perhaps it's all correct. But they miss the point. Tchaikovsky is great not because he took anything from anyone. The great ballet master Marius Petipa also borrowed everywhere. Genius takes from wherever it wants.

I can't explain exactly how music is composed. That's impossible. But it seems to me that I understand something about how Tchaikovsky composed. I can look at the score and see how he does certain things. You can spend your life reading scholarly books and still miss the most important thing in Tchaikovsky's music. To speak about Tchaikovsky, it's not enough to have studied his works. You have to feel his music as if it were your own; you have to talk with Tchaikovsky himself. That's the difference.

Of course, Tchaikovsky is the best source of understanding his own music. He wrote wonderful articles on music and very interesting letters. But over a hundred years have passed since then, and some of Tchaikovsky's ideas and opinions are hard to understand without special commentaries. The world Tchaikovsky lived in no longer exists. I'm not very old, but I still remember that world, which is gone forever. I was born and raised in the old Russia. My teachers were people who knew Tchaikovsky, who talked with him and shared good wine and good cognac, of which he was a connoisseur.

Ballet—it's a very closed thing. Dancers are apart from other people. In old Russia we were even more apart because we were the Imperial Ballet. We studied separately and lived

separately. The old ways are preserved best in a closed world.
There is one more important thing: in ballet we respect tradition. You show something, and then you tell something about
it. In ballet they try hard to remember. That's why dancers
have better memories than other people.

In Russia I always heard stories about Tchaikovsky. I
heard them from those who had worked with Tchaikovsky
and with Petipa. I was born some ten years after Tchaikovsky's death. Petipa died when I was about six years old.
But Tchaikovsky and Petipa were alive for me. And people
around me talked about them as if they were alive. That's why
I feel I can explain a few things about Tchaikovsky's music
and also what he thought about the music of other composers,
and I can comment on Tchaikovsky's opinions on religion and
politics, on the Russian countryside and Western cities. My
life experiences can help me there. I hope that I'm not making
anything up. But, of course, I can't guarantee that I won't make
a mistake. We all make mistakes. I'm not a musicologist, and
I'm not a writer. I'm only an intermediary between Tchaikovsky and those who want to learn more about his music and
to understand it better.

ONE

Tchaikovsky and Balanchine

Y first time on the stage was in a Tchaikovsky ballet. It was in *Sleeping Beauty*. I was still a small boy then. I was Cupid, a tiny Cupid. It was Petipa's choreography. I was set down on a golden cage. And suddenly everything opened! A crowd of people, an elegant audience. And the Maryinsky Theater all light blue and gold! And suddenly the orchestra started playing. I sat on the cage in indescribable ecstasy enjoying it all—the music, the theater, and the fact that I was onstage. Thanks to *Sleeping Beauty* I fell in love with ballet.

I learned all of Tchaikovsky's ballets and his operas, as well. The operas were performed at the Imperial Maryinsky Theater, too. We pupils of the ballet school participated in the ballet scenes of *Eugene Onegin* and *Queen of Spades*.

Sometimes people say to me, "I love the music of such-

George Balanchine, age twelve, as Cupid in The Sleeping Beauty   31

32   and-such composer." My feelings for Tchaikovsky were different, even as a child. Imagine yourself in a church and suddenly the organ starts playing overwhelmingly grand music in
all its registers. And you stand there mouth agape in astonishment. That's how I always felt about Tchaikovsky. He's like a
father to me.

I was small and knew nothing about music theory. But I
liked all of Tchaikovsky's compositions. When I looked at his
pictures, I liked his face. I liked everything about him, everything Tchaikovsky had ever done in his life.

Even though I was small, it seems I was a wizard in some
things. People around me would say, "Tchaikovsky? Eh, not
bad, so-so." At first it bothered me—why, why do they say
that? And then I thought, And who are they to say that? What
have they ever done? Let them say whatever they want! Silly
geese!

I began to learn to make my own judgments. I learned all
these things—a little music theory, some harmony and counterpoint. I played piano, and I started to compose. And I understood what a smart composer Tchaikovsky had been. He is
a composer for wise and subtle listeners. He is a refined artist.

There are lovers of Tchaikovsky who don't understand a
thing about him. I remember, here in America, in San Fran-
cisco, old White Russians coming to see me. They said they
adored Tchaikovsky. But only the Tchaikovsky that can be
sung easily at home: his songs, some things from the operas.
For them that's the real Tchaikovsky. His symphonies and
string quartets—that's "not it." I don't argue with dilettantes
like that; there's no point. To know music, you must study a
bit. Otherwise, how can you ever learn about music?

Tchaikovsky is the greatest Russian composer. But you
could never get all Russians to agree to that. It's not like
Beethoven in Germany where the moment you mention his
name, everyone goes, "Oh yes!" In Germany, millions of pon-

derous books have been written teaching respect for Beetho-
ven. Of course, even there you have a lot of hypocrisy.
Everyone praises Beethoven, saying, "We want to listen to
Beethoven but not this minute. Don't have time right now."

It's hard for people to make the necessary effort to understand Tchaikovsky. Some violinists understand him. Pianists like Tchaikovsky's First Piano Concerto. But the attitude is
"We've played it, and fine, that's enough." No one holds on to
that music. Maybe some dancers do. They love Tchaikovsky
and not only the ballets, but they like to listen to his symphonies as well. I sometimes talk to dancers, still little girls,
and try to explain to them: "Tchaikovsky is a genius! Listen,
just listen to how wonderful his music is!"

You have to listen closely in order to appreciate the
beauty of Tchaikovsky's Fifth Symphony. You have to slow
down, you have to stop and concentrate a bit. But people don't
have time. Everyone's in a hurry. Who pays attention to
music!

Tchaikovsky was never fashionable. During his lifetime
"progressive" Russians felt that he was not Russian enough.
The Germans, on the contrary, felt that his music was too
crude. In Russia, after the revolution, Tchaikovsky was de-
spised; they wrote in the newspapers that his music was pessi-
mistic, decadent, that the proletariat did not need it. For some
reason they felt that the proletariat would like the operas of
Meyerbeer, that they were more appropriate to the "revolutionary moment," as they liked to put it.

Diaghilev produced Tchaikovsky's *Sleeping Beauty* in London in 1921, but no one understood anything there. Diaghilev
almost went bankrupt. When I came to America, they didn't
play Tchaikovsky that much either, except for the two or three
popular symphonies. When I did Tchaikovsky's *Serenade* here,
it turned out that no one knew it. It wasn't played here. And
they didn't play Tchaikovsky's magnificent orchestral suites,

34   the First, Second, or Third. No one knew his *Mozartiana*. Tchaikovsky's piano music wasn't performed at all, except for the First Piano Concerto.

Here, in our theater, we've been presenting Tchaikovsky for years. Almost every season we perform Tchaikovsky at least twenty-five times. We do it all the time. In our repertory we probably have fifteen ballets to music by Tchaikovsky.

And yet the snobs still won't admit that Tchaikovsky is a great composer. And they never will. They will pretend to love Telemann or some other obscure Baroque composer, who wrote a million identical concerti. I think that even if they read this they'll still say, "We don't agree with this at all! We think that Tchaikovsky is a mediocrity!" But what do we care what they think?

By the way, it was the same with Stravinsky and Ravel. They didn't like Ravel either. When I announced our Ravel festival, everyone asked, "Why Ravel?" And one music critic wrote, "Ravel is an absolutely second-rate composer. What are you doing? Why are you playing him? Debussy is much better!"

I don't agree with that opinion. Ravel's opera *L'Enfant et les sortilèges* is a work of genius. But it has to be studied slowly, be relished. Gradually, the public agreed with me that Ravel is a great composer. And they accepted Stravinsky, too. You have to be patient.

Of course, I wasn't alone in working for this. My boys are staging ballets to Tchaikovsky's music. I suggested what to use. Peter Martins will do *Capriccio italien;* Jacques d'Amboise, the *Concert Fantasy* for piano and orchestra. No one ever plays this work even though it has remarkable music. John Taras is working on *Souvenir de Florence*, which is better known than any of Tchaikovsky's splendid string quartets but still not enough. Jerry Robbins has chosen the beautiful piano pieces from the *Seasons* cycle.

And, of course, Tchaikovsky is always with us. I don't want to talk about it; I'm afraid that I'll be misunderstood. Maybe it's not right to talk about it. But it's true. In everything that I did to Tchaikovsky's music, I sensed his help. It wasn't real conversation. But when I was working and saw that something was coming of it, I felt that it was Tchaikovsky who had helped me. Or else he would say don't! Again, that doesn't mean that Tchaikovsky himself really stopped me. But if I saw that a ballet wasn't working, that meant that I should not do it, that in this, Tchaikovsky wouldn't help me. When I was doing *Serenade*, Tchaikovsky encouraged me. Almost the whole *Serenade* is done with his help. I feel that way about Stravinsky, too. When we were preparing the Stravinsky festival, he was with us.

> *This belief in the possibility of a mystical contact with the deceased greats is more prevalent among Russian musicians than among their more rational-minded Western colleagues. [The Russian cellist and conductor] Mstislav Rostropovich said: "When I was invited to conduct Prokofiev's opera* War and Peace *at the Moscow Bolshoi Theater, the management wanted me to fail. They gave me only three rehearsals. I was bound to fail!*
>
> *"On the day of the performance," continues Rostropovich, "I went to Prokofiev's grave outside Moscow. I embraced the headstone, asking Prokofiev to help me. And he did. I'm certain of it because he was the only one who could do it. The performance was a triumphant success."*

Things like that have happened to me. If it's not going well, I ask Tchaikovsky, "Please!" I never saw Tchaikovsky, but I turned to him. I've never spoken about this. It's awkward to speak about it. But alone, without Tchaikovsky's help, I would not have managed. I couldn't do it alone; I'm not smart enough for it.

The sense of having continuing dialogue with their dead predecessors and friends helps Russians overcome the fear of death. For them, the other world is filled with people they know, and therefore it isn't scary. There is a feeling of familiarity, almost coziness. That's why Rostropovich answered the question "Is he afraid of death?" quite firmly: "No! In that life I have a greater balance than in this one. I have more friends there. And I relate with them there on the level of a new, other life. That's why I'm not afraid of death." That feeling of a personal, almost intimate contact with the shades of the great is characteristic of Russians.

It's a Russian trait. But it is also typical of all theater people. You suddenly feel the presence of Tchaikovsky and realize: "Of course, it's him! I'm going to work with him. He'll help me."

Balanchine examining the sets for Adagio Lamentoso, *from Tchaikovsky's Sixth Symphony*

The Tchaikovsky family, 1848: eight-year-old Pierre at far left.

TWO

Childhood

T CHAIKOVSKY loved his mother more than his father. Even when he was a grown man he couldn't talk about her without tears. She died of cholera, when Tchaikovsky was only fourteen. It was an open wound for the rest of his life. And, as we know, death from cholera became an idée fixe for Tchaikovsky. Tchaikovsky's mother was of French extraction. The family called the boy Pierre, though in Russian Pyotr or Petya would have been correct. And in school I was called Georges, even though it should have been Georgy or Yura.

Childhood impressions are almost always the most powerful. This holds particularly for musicians and dancers, because they usually start studying music and ballet at a very early age. We know that Tchaikovsky's parents loved him very much. That is enviable. Everyone wants to be the favorite child in a family, but not everyone has the luck. Tchaikovsky's parents also believed that Pierre would be a remarkable musi- 39

40 cian. And Tchaikovsky himself was certain from childhood
that he would be a famous composer.

> *Pierre's first musical impressions were not of live perfor-*
> *mances but of mechanical sound—as if he were a child of the*
> *late twentieth century. His father bought him a rather large*
> *mechanical organ, and Pierre listened (as he later said, "in*
> *holy rapture") as the organ played excerpts from Mozart's*
> *opera* Don Giovanni. *The organ also played music by Ros-*
> *sini, Bellini, and Donizetti. Tchaikovsky came to love Italian*
> *opera and remained true to it even when serious musicians in*
> *Russia considered Italian music "vulgar."*
>
> *Pierre's early contacts with music were both exhilarat-*
> *ing and traumatic. Five-year-old Pierre was forbidden to*
> *spend too much time at the piano. He continued "to play" by*
> *rapping his fingers on the window pane, breaking it and se-*
> *verely slashing his hand. Then, his parents realized that the*
> *boy had to study music seriously.*
>
> *One night, hearing little Pierre cry, his governess came*
> *up to the nursery and asked what was the matter. "Oh, it's*
> *that music, the music, make it go away! It's here, here," the*
> *boy replied, weeping and pointing at his head. "It won't give*
> *me any peace!"*

Here in America people think that music must bring only
pleasure, must entertain. That, of course, is not so, especially
if you are a professional. Music also brings suffering and a
sense of your own insignificance. It's not always comfortable
to be one-on-one with it. That's why it's more pleasant to listen to music in a concert along with an audience.

A child must be made accustomed to music very carefully
and cautiously. It must be explained to him that this is serious
business. Tchaikovsky's governess was good, she helped him
with the music. He also mastered French with her. My family,

Tchaikovsky, 1859

on the other hand, had a German bonne, whom I liked very much. I was very small then. And then she left. When I entered ballet school, we had servants there. But that was something different. I still recall my bonne with tenderness.

My parents stuck me in ballet school when I was small. In just the same way young Tchaikovsky's parents stuck him in the School of Jurisprudence, also in St. Petersburg. And they

42   left for more than two years. Pierre suffered terribly. I can understand that because I also was homesick. But it was easier
for me—my parents lived nearby in Lounatiokki, in Finland.
On Sundays my aunt sometimes came over and picked me up
at school and took me home for the day. She lived in Petersburg.

> Many years later Tchaikovsky recalled his life in the School
> of Jurisprudence: On Thursdays in the school's dining hall
> the pupils were given borsch, bitki (ground meat patties), and
> buckwheat kasha. The smell of the borsch and kasha plea-
> santly tickled the nose, and in anticipation of the bitki,
> Tchaikovsky's soul "was moved." There were only two days
> left until Saturday, when you could visit your relatives.

At our school we also had borsch and bitki, and kasha on
Thursday. The bitki were served in sour cream sauce, delicious! And the borsch was a work of genius! On Saturdays at
our school, too, many children went home. Friday was the day
at the steambath. And on Saturday the school was deserted,
for two days. It was sad and lonely to be left. You'd go to
church and stand there for some time. The school had a
chapel. The master would be there with maybe two or three
other students. You had to kill time before dinner. I would go
to the reception hall and play the piano. There was no one
there, total emptiness. Then came dinner, and after dinner,
bed.

We could read before going to sleep. I liked reading Jules
Verne—*Twenty Thousand Leagues Under the Sea*, *The Mysterious
Island*. I still remember the captions under the pictures: "If we
hear bells at night in the open sea, that means the ship has
sunk."

We were also enthralled by the adventures of Sherlock
Holmes, Nick Carter, and Pinkerton. They came out serially,

in colored cardboard covers. Every week you could buy the next installment, several dozen pages. It was cheap—ten or twelve kopeks. We ate up those books and passed them along. I remember *Pinkerton's Journey to the Other World, The Murdering Model*, and *The Mystery of the Burgas Castle*. Very entertaining!

> In his youth, Tchaikovsky enjoyed the adventure literature of his day: Eugène Sue, Alexandre Dumas père, Frederic Soulier (Memoirs of the Devil), and Paul Féval. Later he was a fan of the novels of Louis Jacolio; Tchaikovsky described them as being "very entertainingly written books." Tchaikovsky's governess recalled the first books she read with Pierre: "Besides Education Maternelle by Mlle Amable Tastu, we also had Family Education by Miss Edgeworth in several volumes. For natural history we had a small illustrated volume by Buffon. One particularly beloved volume, which we read and talked about on Saturday evenings, was Famous Children by Michel Mason." They also read Les Petits Musiciens by Eugenie Foa. In one of his letters little Pierre reports that he is reading the letters of Mme de Sévigné and Le Génie du Christianisme by Chateaubriand, but admits that he "understands nothing."

I also had marvelous children's books but different; they were about the adventures of *murzilki*. They were tiny, like the head of a pin, those *murzilki*. They could get in anywhere and see everything. No one knows about *murzilki* here, and I think it would be good for American children to learn about them. Their story should be translated into English and then made into a cartoon show for television. It would be marvelous. I also remember books about *Styopka-Rastryopka* (unkempt Styopka). That was a translation from the German of Dr. Hoffmann's *Struwelpeter*—not the Hoffmann who wrote *The Nutcracker*, another one. He did the pictures, too. They were

44   interesting, cruel books. I remember that poor Styopka, in
punishment for being so dirty, had his fingers as well as his
nails cut off by the barber. And, of course, there was the unforgettable *Max und Moritz* by Wilhelm Busch! I remember
how they broke into a bakery, they were terrors, those Kat-
zenjammer kids. I really liked Busch, and incidentally, so did
Stravinsky. Stravinsky, even when he was quite advanced in
age, could recite large chunks of Busch by heart.

> *Tchaikovsky wrote, "It seems to me that the delight elicited
> by art and literature in early youth leaves its mark on your
> entire life and is of great significance. . . ."*

He heard Mozart in his childhood, and Mozart remained a god
for Tchaikovsky. He heard Glinka and fell in love for life. And
he was touchingly loyal: Tchaikovsky heard Glinka's *Life for
the Tsar* before his other opera, *Ruslan and Lyudmila;* and for
that reason Tchaikovsky preferred *Life for the Tsar!* (At first, I
had preferred *Life* myself. But after the revolution they completely stopped performing the opera because of its monarchist story. Thus I came to know *Ruslan and Lyudmila* better
and started to love it.) In *Life for the Tsar,* a peasant saves the
Russian tsar. Tchaikovsky was stunned when revolutionary
terrorists killed Emperor Alexander II. He grew quite close to
the new monarch, Alexander III. Diaghilev said to me that
Alexander III could be counted among the best Russian tsars.
For Russian culture he was, perhaps, really the best of the
Russian monarchs. It was in his reign that Russian literature,
art, music, and ballet began to flourish. Everything that later
made Russia famous began under Alexander III! He was, they
told me, a man of enormous height. Stravinsky saw Alexander
III a few times when he was a child. The emperor was a real
bogatyr, a gigantic warrior, bearded, with a loud voice, and a
penetrating glance. But with Tchaikovsky, for example, he was

always very simple and gentle. The emperor liked Tchaikovsky's music very much. It was he who insisted that Tchaikovsky's opera *Eugene Onegin* be produced at the Imperial Theater in St. Petersburg. No one wanted to do that! The musicians were against it. They envied Tchaikovsky and said that it was a bad opera, untheatrical; the public wouldn't like it. But the tsar gave his order, and the musicians had to obey.

In a letter to Nadezhda von Meck, his wealthy patron of many years and longtime correspondent, Tchaikovsky describes a performance of Eugene Onegin *in the presence of the imperial family: "The Emperor wished to see me. He chatted with me a very long time [and] was extremely kind and amiable toward me. [He] inquired with greatest sympathy and in minute detail about my life and my musical affairs, after which he brought me to the Empress, who in her turn treated me with touching attention."*

Tchaikovsky composed the Coronation March and the Coronation Cantata for Alexander III. In payment, the tsar gave him a diamond ring. And later he granted Tchaikovsky a pension of three thousand rubles a year for life. An enormous sum in those days! But even more importantly, Tchaikovsky's operas and ballets were produced with no expenses spared, because the funds came from the imperial treasury. Tchaikovsky did not have to make the rounds of the wealthy, hat in hands, humiliating himself, begging for a ruble here, a ruble there. His works were produced at the Imperial Theater! Tchaikovsky believed in God and the tsar from childhood. At the age of seven Pierre composed a poem to his guardian angel—in French!

When Pierre lived at the school, the Metropolitan said the liturgy on St. Catherine's Day every year. Tchaikovsky re-

*called that in his childhood he had a lovely soprano and for
several years in a row sang first soprano in sacred trios for
the Metropolitan at the beginning and at the end of the liturgy: "The liturgy had a profound poetic effect on me."*

The Metropolitan came to their church on St. Catherine's Day
because the memory of Catherine the Great was revered in
Russia. The liturgy made a wonderful impression on me when
I was a child, too. The priests came out—all dressed opulently
in gorgeous miters, looking just like saints. And the service itself is so touching and beautiful. The boys in the church choir
sing so delicately, like angels. I always envied them. I wanted
so badly to sing in a church choir. But I had to wait for my
voice to change. Other boys sang—older ones—from the ballet school. And then, after the revolution, when I was old
enough, our school no longer had a church choir.

*Tchaikovsky often said how much he loved the Russian Or-
thodox church services but that it seemed to him that some of
the Orthodox rituals were too long. He wrote to his brother
Modest once on this topic: "I was at a service preparing
chrism, the bringing out of the* plashchanitsa *at Uspensky
Cathedral, at the Paschal Matins in the Church of Christ
the Saviour, and the Vespers on the first day of Easter (and
many other services) there. I always came away with the impression of piety, splendor, and beauty. But unfortunately,
every time the impression was marred by the extremely
dragged-out nature of our service. Alas! I must speak the
truth: there is much that is excessive, which lengthens the
service with no need, wearying the most stubborn attention,
cooling the most ardent feelings. If the Orthodox service requires any reforms—it is certainly in that sense."*

Of course, of course, it's too long, too long! They wave and
wave the censers. And read and read. And keep repeating the

same things: "Let us pray unto the Lord"—"Lord have   47
mercy"—"Let us pray unto the Lord"—"Lord have mercy."
The Easter service in the Orthodox Church is very long. We
would be at St. Vladimir's church in Petersburg for four hours.
I'd come at the very beginning with my aunt and mother, and
we stood throughout the whole service on the stone floor. Four
hours on a stone floor!

Tchaikovsky talks about preparing the chrism. I have to
explain what it is. They take olive oil, grape wine, and various
aromatic substances and prepare a special mixture called *miro*,
or chrism, which is then blessed in a special rite. This is a sacred mystery that recalls the Pentecost. We know that the
Holy Spirit came down to the apostles, thereby creating the
Church from them. Everyone who is christened is anointed by
the chrism. It is a very important thing.

And I can explain the *plashchanitsa* Tchaikovsky writes
about, too. It's also called Epitaphia, and it symbolizes the
body of Christ. It's a cloth, velvet or of precious fabric, on
which is depicted the body of Christ removed from the Cross.
It is brought out from the altar into the middle of the church
and set upon a pedestal decorated with flowers. For us this
symbolizes the removal of Christ from the Cross so that the
people can worship Him.

And naturally I remember the Vespers in St. Petersburg,
the first day of Easter. At first everyone stands there, waiting.
Then the priests come out slowly, the service begins. And then
it gets merrier: the choir starts to sing, the altar attendants
walk around. The choir sings, "Christ is risen from the dead,
trampling down death by death, and upon those in the tombs
bestowing life." The Metropolitan blesses the people. In St.
Vladimir's in Petersburg, I remember, they opened up the
altar. At Easter the opening of the altar is a miraculous event.
Then the service is over, the doors of the altar are shut, and it
grows dark.

Nikolsky Cathedral

Tchaikovsky wrote to von Meck: "Every hour and every minute I thank God that He gave me faith in Him. With my cowardice and ability to plunge so far in spirit at the slightest push that I strive for nonexistence—*what would come of me if I did not believe in God and did not give myself up to His will?"*

It is very important that Tchaikovsky and I are of the the same
Church. I know that Tchaikovsky had real faith. I do not see
many people today who have real faith. Because it is very difficult. You must not only obey some rules, you must believe
that the Son of God was born, suffered, and was resurrected.
And believe that He rose to the Heavens. And will come a second time to earth. Religion is primarily faith, and people today
are used to treating everything skeptically, mockingly. That
cannot be. You can't test faith.

I'm sometimes asked, "How is it that you are a believer?"
You can't come to faith suddenly, just out of the blue. You
have to achieve faith from childhood, step-by-step. That's how
Tchaikovsky did it, that's how Stravinsky did it. They read the
Gospels from childhood, memorizing them. The words of the
New Testament are rooted in all of us. We were all christened,
anointed with *miro*, taken to church; we took Communion.
You can't plunge into faith, like diving into a swimming pool.
You have to enter it gradually, like going into the ocean. You
have to start doing it in early childhood.

THREE

St. Petersburg

F OR me, Tchaikovsky is a St. Petersburg composer, absolutely Petersburgian. And not only because he studied in Petersburg, graduating from the conservatory and living there a long time. And not only because he himself considered it his hometown and said so. Much more importantly, in the essence of his music, Tchaikovsky is a Petersburger, just as Pushkin and Stravinsky were Petersburgers.

It is difficult to explain, but I will try, because it is important and needs explaining. And perhaps I will manage to do it, because I myself am a Petersburger; I was born and raised in St. Petersburg.

First of all, Petersburg is a very original city, one that resembles no other. It was built in an unusual way: all at once, as if it arose miraculously. Tsar Peter the Great gave the order—and it sprang up! That's why Petersburg had straight, beautiful streets. And they always were concerned with proportion there. There was a special imperial decree that the height of

52   the buildings could not exceed the width of the streets. For instance, I lived on the famous Theater Street, next to the Alexandrinsky Imperial Theater. A small street, but of extraordinary beauty, and why is that? The length of the street is 220 meters, the width 22 meters, and the height of the buildings on the street is also 22 meters. It's not hard to figure out why the street is so fantastic!

The Russian tsars were so rich that they imported the best architects of Europe to St. Petersburg—from Italy, Austria, France. They paid them enormous sums. And obviously the Romanov dynasty understood beauty. In the Romanov vein there was a strong admixture of German blood; beginning with Peter the Great, they married German women. But you won't find Germanic architecture in Petersburg. All the buildings are elegant, light—that's the Italian or Austrian style. And even the tsars' residence, the Winter Palace, is in the light Italo-Austrian style. It's called *Petersburg Empire*—elegant, simple, refined. Without pretension, but majestic. That's what Petersburg is.

For me, Petersburg is inseparable from Pushkin, Russia's greatest poet. Pushkin described the city exquisitely in his poetry and prose and thereby increased its beauty. Starting in childhood, we all perceived Petersburg through the prism of Pushkin's poetry. I don't know of any other such situation, with the exception perhaps of Florence and Dante. Pushkin's poetry is light, majestic, and balanced—like Petersburg, like Mozart's music. Petersburg is a European city that arose in Russia by miracle. And Pushkin is the miracle of Russian literature: he is a European from Russia. Tchaikovsky was also a Russian European; that is why he loved Pushkin so much. He wrote his three best operas to works by Pushkin—*Mazeppa*, *Eugene Onegin*, and *The Queen of Spades*. And, of course, there's another example of a European from Russia, Igor Fyodorovich Stravinsky.

The Winter Palace

Young Tchaikovsky wrote to his sister: "Everything that is dear to my heart is in St. Petersburg, and without it life for me is positively impossible. And there, when my pockets are not too empty, my heart rejoices. . . . Do you know my weakness? When I do have money in my pocket, I give it all to pleasure; that is vile, that is stupid—I know; strictly speaking, I cannot have money for pleasure; I have incommensurate debts that demand payment, I have urgent needs that should take priority—but I (once again through weakness) disdain all that and enjoy myself. Such is my character."

How like Mozart! You can see the man and the city here. The man is a real artist! And the city, a marvelous place for an artist! That's the way I always lived: If I have money I spend it and have a good time; if I don't have it, I don't worry too

Nevsky Prospect

much. It's a pleasure to walk around St. Petersburg, even when you have no money at all. Tchaikovsky once said that even if things were going badly, all his rubles gone, unhappy in love—when he felt like crying!—if he strolled down Nevsky Prospect and back up, his soul felt good again. Pure Mozart! And it's true, Nevsky Prospect is a splendid place to walk; it's straight and filled with festive crowds, restaurants, theaters. But it's also good to walk along Nevsky during the white nights when it's empty.

White nights are another marvel of St. Petersburg. White nights come in spring. The sun sets, and then suddenly a strange white light appears, as if through translucent glass. That's the northern lights. Everything seems eerie.

Fortress of Peter and Paul

> *Tchaikovsky wrote about the white nights: "I can't sleep in this incredible combination of nocturnal quiet and daytime light."*

We young people also could not sleep; we stayed out a lot on white nights; we'd go look at the famous Sphinxes at the Academy of Art. They are three thousand years old, they were brought at the tsar's orders from Egypt. We'd go over the bridge to the Fortress of Peter and Paul. We'd be in a group, boys and girls. When I play Tchaikovsky's music, I recall those white nights. They're not southern nights, Italian, when the stars sparkle and the music is loud. No, they were modest, unobtrusive, you had to feel them.

56   I was lucky, I was born in the Petersburg that Tchaikovsky had walked in. There was still a lot left of the old St. Petersburg of the 1880s. Then the city began changing rapidly. And, of course, it became totally different after the revolution. So you might say that I lived in three different cities. And each was Petersburg in its own way.

      Sometimes cholera would remind us of Tchaikovsky's St. Petersburg. Suddenly posters would appear on the buildings' walls—don't drink tap water, don't eat raw fruits and vegetables. The odor of carbolic acid was everywhere. In ballet school the older students told us that in earlier days the school would sometimes be shut because of the cholera.

      In our day they closed the school only if it was very cold, eighteen degrees below Reaumur. People lit bonfires in the streets. But usually no one bothers about the weather in Russia. If it's warm, it's warm; if it's cold, it's cold, but as for how many degrees—it doesn't matter, no one cares. (It's only here in the West that everyone worries about the exact number of degrees, and after it's announced people know whether they're hot or cold.)

      And, of course, there were people around who had known Tchaikovsky. For instance, Pavel Gerdt, who had been the very first Desiré in the ballet *Sleeping Beauty* and the very first Prince Coqueluche in *The Nutcracker*. He was incredible— he danced in the Maryinsky Theater until he was seventy. A handsome man, very imposing. He did not like to be asked about his age, he was strict. There was another old man, just the opposite, small and friendly, easygoing, with a gray mustache, Riccardo Drigo, a conductor from Italy; we called him Richard Yevgenievich. He spoke a very funny Russian. Drigo had conducted the premieres of both *The Nutcracker* and *Sleeping Beauty*. He had discussed the music and tempi with Tchaikovsky himself! Even in our day he conducted ballet performances in the Maryinsky. Drigo was not at all a bad composer. We did his *Harlequinade* in New York; the public liked it.

I didn't see Marius Petipa. He had died by the time I went to school but not long before that. They still remembered him, told many stories about him. Without Petipa, of course, Tchaikovsky's ballets would not be the same thing.

The composer Alexander Konstantinovich Glazunov, a friend of Tchaikovsky's and director of the St. Petersburg Conservatory, came to our theater to play his ballet *Raymonda* on the piano. We rehearsed, and Glazunov played. He loved to play the piano, he was excellent. I was told that Glazunov had never studied piano, but you couldn't tell. He played beautifully, fluidly, clearly. It was just right for ballet rehearsal.

Of course, I met people later who had known Tchaikovsky: the artist Alexandre Benois, Prince Argutinsky. Diaghilev had known Tchaikovsky. They were very distant relatives, and so he liked to call Tchaikovsky "Uncle Petya." Diaghilev once told me that in his youth he wrote a violin sonata dedicated to Tchaikovsky. Laughing, he said it was terrible junk.

And, of course, old St. Petersburg was a city of eccentrics. They gave it color and flavor. I used to know one such eccentric quite well—Levky Ivanovich Zheverzheyev. I married his daughter, Tamara, in Russia. Zheverzheyev was not yet old. He was very clever and rich.

The famous director Vsevolod Meyerhold wrote this about Zheverzheyev: "The city of Peter—St. Petersburg—Petrograd (as it is called now)—only it, only its air, its stones, its canals are capable of creating people like Zheverzheyev. To live and die in St. Petersburg! What happiness."

Oh, yes, Zheverzheyev was definitely a Petersburger, absolutely! He owned a brocade mill and a church-supply store on

Zheverzheyev, left, with V. Meyerhold and Yu. Shaporin

Nevsky Prospect. He built a theater on Troitskaya Street. At Zheverzheyev's factory they made vestments and miters for the patriarch and other higher clergy. It took a whole year, I think, to make a roll of gold brocade. A whole year! The brocade was heavy, thick, of pure gold. That's what they put on the patriarch! I had a friend, the pianist Nikolai Kopeikin. In Russia before the revolution the Kopeikins owned a button factory. The whole Russian army had metal buttons and on each one was stamped "Kopeikin." They also made medals, orders, badges, and crosses and other church ornaments out of gold. And whenever they had an important order, they said at the Kopeikin factory, "Well, we have another order from the Zheverzheyevs." That meant, the Zheverzheyevs had ordered a gold cross or something like that.

Zheverzheyev had a marvelous library: first editions only, thousands of rare books. They were kept in Zheverzheyev's enormous apartment on Grafsky Alley. Twenty-five rooms! He owned the whole building. I heard a story going around that it was Zheverzheyev's idea that Tamara and I get married. Nothing of the kind, it never happened. Zheverzheyev paid no attention to Tamara and me, he was totally engrossed in his unique collection. I lived at the Zheverzheyev house; I had nowhere else to go. There was a wonderful piano there. Zheverzheyev loved Wagner, he had all his scores. And he always said, "Please, sit down and play something of Wagner's." I played; of course, nothing where there is singing, all those difficult ensembles, but more often the introductions and overtures. Zheverzheyev demanded Wagner from me, that's true. But to marry Tamara, no. Tamara and I got married on our own.

The St. Petersburg of my childhood was a big, noisy city. The double-decker horse cars, which Tchaikovsky rode, were replaced by streetcars. There were electric streetlights instead of gas ones. The telephone appeared and so did steam heat. I was born in that city. When I was small our bonne took us to play on Poklonnaya Hill. There were three ponds there. We played in Suvorov Garden. (We lived on Suvorov Prospect, across from the Academy.) Our bonne took us walking along the embankment of the Neva, and we waited impatiently for the cannon at the Fortress of Peter and Paul to boom at noon. We went to the zoo. Tchaikovsky really liked the Petersburg Zoo, he often went there. He especially enjoyed the frolicking bear cubs. But Tchaikovsky felt sorry for the lions and tigers. And it's true, lions and tigers behind bars look pathetic. They should be seen in the movies, instead.

Then I was stuck in ballet school; its full name was the Imperial Saint Petersburg Theatrical School. I lived and was raised there, without seeing my mother or father. We were taken "on account"—that is, full board and tuition at the expense of the royal treasury. There, at the school, we studied,

60   ate, and slept, everything. We rehearsed ballets in the large rehearsal hall. And we had our own small theater there, and a
chapel, and an infirmary. We were all Petersburgers, those of
us who were brought up at that school. Because this was a
court school! We had special uniforms—light blue, very
handsome; silver lyres on our collars and caps—and we were
driven around in carriages. Two men in livery sat on the
coachbox! Like *Cinderella!* . . . And we were presented to Nicholas II, son of Alexander III, Tchaikovsky's patron. That was
December 6, St. Nicholas' Day, the tsar's name day. That day
(and on the name day of the empress) we had special services
in the school chapel, and we were given delicious hot chocolate. Nicholas II loved the ballet *The Little Humpbacked Horse.* He
particularly liked the march at the end of the ballet, a German
march. It was put in there especially for him, and all of us
children participated in that march. And then we changed and
went in pairs, boys and girls, to see the emperor. With a master and mistress from school. The girls first, I think, and then
the boys, in uniform, hands at our sides.

Everyone thinks that the tsar's box at the Maryinsky Theater is in the middle. But actually, it was on the side, on the
right. It had a separate entrance, a separate foyer, with a large
private driveway. When you come in, it's like a colossal apartment: chandeliers, the walls covered in light blue. The emperor sat there with his whole family—Empress Alexandra
Feodorovna, the heir, his daughters—and we would be lined
up by size and presented: Efimov, Balanchivadze, Mikhailov.
The tsar was not tall. The tsaritsa was a very tall, beautiful
woman. She was dressed sumptuously. The grand princesses,
Nicholas' daughters, were also beauties. The tsar had protrud-
ing light-colored eyes, and he rolled his Rs. If he said, "Well,
how are you?" we were supposed to click our heels and reply,
"Highly pleased, Your Imperial Majesty!" We were given
chocolate in silver boxes, wonderful ones! And the mugs were

Balanchine's graduation class, 1921, at the Maryinsky Ballet School: Balan-chine second from right; first woman on right is Lida Ivanova.

exquisite, porcelain with light blue lyres and the imperial monogram. I didn't save any of it. At the time, it was all rather unimportant to me.

And how wonderful it was to be under imperial patron-age, as the whole ballet was. We didn't have to look for money from rich merchants or bankers. That's why Petipa could stage Tchaikovsky's ballets so luxuriously. It took enormous amounts of money to do so! And all the tsar wanted in return was to play the march from *The Little Humpbacked Horse*.

It was good that our tsar had respect for art and music. That was the tsarist tradition, and it benefited Tchaikovsky

The Maryinsky Theater

and other great Russian musicians, as well as the ballet. We were all the tsar's dependents. We had servants and lackeys at the school: all handsome men in uniform, buttoned from top to bottom. We got up, washed, dressed, and took off. We didn't make the beds, we left everything. The servants took care of it.

There were about thirty of us in the room. A large room! Only boys; the girls were on another floor. We were all in love with the grown-up ballerinas, the soloists of the Maryinsky Theater. We didn't have "affairs" with the girls from the school; it was hard to meet—they were watched by the class ladies and the maids. And, most important, we were busy all the time and got very tired. So we didn't feel any particular desire for the girls.

When it was time to perform at the Maryinsky Theater— they gave ballets Wednesdays and Sundays, but we also performed in the operas—those were good days. The ones who went home on Saturdays came back. We were seated six at a time in the carriage—a marvelous coach, which we called Noah's Ark—and brought straight to the theater. On Sundays we had a good dinner—beef patties with macaroni, my favorite. I also liked pickles. And once a week we had apricot pies; we were given the best! We sometimes had *rakhat-lukum* and halvah, but rarely: Eastern sweets rot the teeth.

The worst day was Monday: get up at seven, wash in the icy water in the basin . . . Brrrrr . . . And straight to work! Besides ballet and music classes, we had regular subjects, too, like other schools: math, history, geography, literature, and French. I was good at math. And our mathematics teacher was excellent. He was forty-five (at the time I thought he was ancient), a good, kind man. In the upper classes they teased him, they liked doing it. There was one idiot who played the clown: he was always smudged with ink, and he was obnoxious and rude. He stuck his tongue out at the teacher and everyone laughed. The mathematician wept at this, and we felt sorry for him. We younger boys never mocked him, we were well disciplined.

History and literature I liked less. Literature seemed like such a long thing to me, you couldn't learn it all at once. We memorized Pushkin, Lermontov, Griboyedov. At first I thought that I was forgetting it all immediately. But now, so many decades later, it turns out I remember a lot! I also liked religion classes. Tchaikovsky, when he was at school, loved religion best.

We studied classic dance with Samuel Konstantinovich

64 Andrianov. He was a handsome man, tall, and a brilliant teacher. But we did not study with him long; Andrianov died quite young, from galloping consumption. Andrianov also staged ballets; at the time they seemed interesting to me. He considered us insects, of course. Andrianov was a marvelous Siegfried in *Swan Lake*.

We were taught ballroom dancing by Nikolai Ludvigovich Gavlikovsky. I liked this very much, too. He taught us traditional things: *passpied, chassé*, and of course the mazurka and polonaise.

We had real classical technique, pure. In Moscow they did not teach in the same way, their ballet dancers were brought up differently. In Moscow they had more running around on the stage naked, like show-offs, flexing their muscles. In Moscow, there was much more acrobatics. Not the Imperial style at all. And that made sense—after all, the tsar lived in our city. Petersburg is Versailles. Or the Île-de-France! Tchaikovsky, even though he lived in Moscow and taught there (they stupidly did not ask him to teach at the Petersburg Conservatory, so he moved to the Moscow Conservatory), he did not like Moscow, called it an alien city.

> *Tchaikovsky wrote to Nadezhda von Meck: "Petersburg, compared to Moscow, is such a musical city! I hear music here every day. There's nothing comparable in Moscow."*

Of course not! People loved music more in Petersburg than in Moscow.

> *It's not difficult to find innumerable complaints about Moscow in Tchaikovsky's letters: Moscow makes Tchaikovsky feel "dreary and depressed"; Moscow, in his opinion, has too many beggars in the streets (the Moscow beggars, he said, "completely ruined" his walks); in the summer Moscow "is*

totally uninhabitable"; it is "stuffy, dusty, and disgusting."
And, finally, Tchaikovsky is always complaining about the
vile stench of the Moscow streets.

Well, he's exaggerating there, I suppose. I'd been to Moscow a
few times in my youth. My impressions, I remember, were
these: Fancy! Big! Colossal! It looks like a Russian lady who's
become a queen. And she's been all dressed up, in silks, furs,
and diamonds. Moscow is a beautiful, well-born woman.

But Tchaikovsky's brother Modest, to whom he was very
close, lived in Petersburg. And there were many young people
from Petersburg high society whom Tchaikovsky liked. They
understood him, loved his music, revered him. They were
soulmates. They were all interesting, brilliant people, true Petersburgers. After all, St. Petersburg was not only the imperial
capital, it was also the intellectual capital of Russia. That must
be understood. And even after the revolution, when the new
government moved to Moscow, Petersburg remained a European city in Russia. Anna Akhmatova, the famous poet and
beauty, lived there. I was introduced to her. I loved her poetry,
I have it. And as for Mikhail Kuzmin, another great poet, I actually worked with him. Kuzmin was also a very good composer; he wrote the music for *Poor Eugen* (*Hinkemann*) based on
the play by the German expressionist Ernst Toller. It was
staged at the Alexandrinsky Theater by the famous avant-
garde director Sergei Radlov, and I did the dances. Kuzmin
was very concerned that I understand how the accents fell in
his music.

Kuzmin, I think, was the first in Russia to publish verse
and prose about homosexual love. He was a small, skinny old
man with enormous eyes. Very nice, refined, pure charm.
Once, probably, he had dressed quite elegantly. But after the
revolution it was hard to keep your clothes in shape. And yet
Kuzmin always managed to look exquisite. He played the

Mikhail Kuzmin

piano well and loved E. T. A. Hoffmann and Mozart. He played Hoffmann's music for me (not many know it!) and regretted that it resembled Beethoven more than Mozart. I didn't understand all of it in those days. I was only nineteen. But I remember Kuzmin very well.

When the tsar was overthrown, it did not affect the ballet world at first. Religion was still taught at the school. The only sign was that the portrait of Nicholas II was removed. The ushers at the Maryinsky Theater stopped wearing their handsome uniforms, because the uniforms were embroidered with epaulets with the two-headed eagle—the heraldic sign of the empire. The eagles and crowns were removed and knocked down everywhere. In Petersburg, of course, there were disturbances and shooting. It was dangerous to walk the streets, and at school we were told, "Don't walk on such-and-such street." They suggested we keep close to the buildings, so as not to be hit by stray bullets.

Then the Bolsheviks came into power. They say that on October 25, 1917, the first day after the Bolshevik uprising, they were performing *The Nutcracker* at the Maryinsky—perhaps I was in it, I don't recall. The school was shut down for a time but then reopened. Of course, there were fewer pupils. From the large dorm we moved to a smaller room. There was no fuel. It was cold. And the food became very poor.

We still took part in performances, but we were no longer taken to the theater by carriage; they drove us in long sledges. They got rid of them later, too. But the worst part, of course, was being hungry.

Naturally, the school chapel was closed. The calendar was changed; everything was moved thirteen days forward. That was the right thing to do. Russia was thirteen days behind the rest of the world because our church, the Orthodox one, remained on the Julian calendar instead of the Gregorian, like the rest of the world. I celebrate Christmas and other holidays, including New Year's, on the New Style calendar, even though some old Russians stubbornly celebrate the New Year on January 13. That's nonsense, of course!

And one more change. Before the revolution, we were taught to write the old way, with the letter *yat'*. But the Soviets did away with that letter and made other orthographic

68 changes. So now I write without the *yat'*. While Stravinsky always wrote the old way, with the *yat'*, his whole life. That's because he learned to write long before the revolution. It's a question of habit. I was right in-between, neither fish nor fowl. Of course, it doesn't matter how you write, as long as it comes out well. In matters like this I don't cling to the past, like some of those senile toadstools.

There were changes at our Maryinsky Theater, too. The old public fled abroad or hid away. The new one was not particularly interested in classical ballet. We had soldiers and sailors come. They smoked in the theater, ate sunflower seeds, tapped their heavy boots in time to the music. They sat on the railings of the boxes, legs dangling; they thought that very *chic*. The theater stopped being the Imperial Theater, naturally. Many committees sprang up immediately; the orchestra musicians had their own, so did the choir members, even the carpenters. The carpenter's committee decided which ballets to put on: they usually voted for the ones with the easiest sets.

Then the soldiers and sailors got tired of coming to the Maryinsky. They couldn't even warm up there as before: the management stopped heating the place because there was no fuel. The water froze in the pipes and they burst. Ice floated in the sinks. The corps de ballet wore long-sleeved T-shirts under their costumes. But what could the poor prima dancers do? They got pneumonia, one after the other. And they tried to leave for Europe at the first opportunity. Things got so bad that the authorities wanted to close down the theater. A commissar came from Moscow with the orders: everyone was to be fired, and the opera and the ballet were to be disbanded. I was in the ballet troupe by then and was terribly worried. Anatoly Lunacharsky, people's commissar of education and culture, stepped in for us. He truly was a cultured man. With his help, the theater was left alone, but the salaries were very low. It wasn't enough to live on, even very modestly.

In order to make a little money for food, we formed concert troupes; someone sang, someone played the violin, someone read poetry, we danced. We appeared wherever we
could—the city and the suburbs. In Pavlovsk, in Tsarskoe Selo
[Tsar's Village]—marvelous spots! Pavlovsk is a resort area
near Petersburg. In Tchaikovsky's day the "owner" there was
Grand Duke Konstantin Romanov, a poet and a great friend of
Tchaikovsky's. Tchaikovsky loved to come to Pavlovsk in the
summer to listen to good music and enjoy the magnificent Italian architecture. It's much easier to understand *Sleeping Beauty*
if you've seen the beauty and harmony of Pavlovsk. We lived
in Tsarskoe Selo in Soviet times. We occupied the abandoned
houses of the Yousoupoff princes. We set up beds and lived
together; it was fun! There was a large ballroom with a mirror
where we could practice dancing; a glorious garden. Boys and
girls fell in love, because we had more time and less supervi-
sion. I fell in love with Olya Mungalova, who later danced in
Fyodor Lopukhov's "Dance Symphony" and in our "Young
Ballet." She had exquisitely beautiful legs. Every acrobatic
trick was a snap for her.

We performed everywhere, even at the circus. Tchaikovsky liked to go to the circus, incidentally. He loved things
like that: music halls, cabarets. We did a Hindu dance at the
circus, and for every performance we got a loaf of bread.
When I was small I sometimes went to Chinizelli's Circus in
Petersburg. I never thought that I'd ever appear in one myself.
In other places we'd be given a sack of grain or flour, sometimes even a hunk of bacon. If they liked our performance we
might have gotten a tip of a few lumps of sugar. That was a
real bonus, like a high honor. Our most popular piece was a
sailor's dance which we called "Matelot." Danilova, Efimov,
and I portrayed ship's lads who climb an imaginary mast or
unfurled sails to polka music. This was not high art, of course,
but we tried to do it merrily and professionally. Otherwise we

70   might not have gotten any food at all, only money, *sovznaks*, which were worthless. You couldn't buy anything with those bits of paper.

The best payment came at private evenings at the homes of bigshot Communists: there we got American canned goods, all kinds of food from the West. The Americans were sending aid to the starving in Russia. And, as usual, a significant portion of the food landed in the bosses' larders. I remember we got pâté there; it was tasty.

At the Maryinsky Theater, interesting things were going on. Ballet master Fyodor Lopukhov, our new director, staged his famous "Dance Symphony" *Grandeur of the Universe*, to music by Beethoven, and I danced in it. What Lopukhov did was amazing for that time. He was inspired by literature and painting, but it was basically pure dance, real choreography. You could say it was a work of genius! Others tried to come up with something interesting, but it was nonsense, only Lopukhov was a true genius. He treated me well, moved me ahead. Others stood around and criticized Lopukhov, but not I; I tried, I worked with him, I learned from him.

That was my third Petersburg. Don't think that all we did was shiver with cold and hunger. No, we had fun, we went to the movies. I loved going to the movies. We called movies "strips" then. In my school days we did not go to the movies very much, the authorities felt they were not suitable—all kinds of melodramas, like something in four parts "about the adventures of a former beauty in the dregs of society." Also, there weren't that many movie theaters. But then they began bringing in Western films. I particularly liked the German ones, from the UFA Studio, with Conrad Veidt and Werner Krauss. The fox-trot became popular. They danced it not only at parties, but onstage, too. The public loved it, but I didn't— no one really knew how to dance the fox-trot. They made

something up, jumped about like idiots and called it a fox-trot.
But it had nothing to do with the real thing.

At home, at parties, we danced everything, improvising. It was fun. It was hard to get decent clothes. But we tried to dress tastefully.

So I saw Petersburg in different forms, at least three different cities: the old one, then the city of my childhood, and finally Petersburg after the revolution. I saw Petersburg festive and brilliant and almost deserted, I saw it happy and grim. But it was always, no matter how often its name was changed [first St. Petersburg, then Petrograd, and now Leningrad], a great city for me.

I am often asked, "What is your nationality, Russian or Georgian?" And I sometimes think, by blood I am Georgian, by culture, Russian, but by nationality, Petersburgian. Being Petersburgian is not the same thing as being Russian, a "Russky." Petersburg was always a European city, cosmopolitan. Tchaikovsky is also a Petersburger; that's why his music cannot be called "Russky," even though many of his melodies are Russian. That's why I would call Tchaikovsky a great composer from Russia.

In Petersburg lived the people who were dearest to Tchaikovsky; he studied there, and he died and was buried there. Tchaikovsky's music reflects the architecture of Petersburg, its proportions, the Italian and Mozartean spirit of that city. It is an elegant, cosmopolitan city, where life could be fun. But people there understood art and knew how to work hard, without sparing themselves. Petersburgers were polite people, but unpretentious, without the British punctiliousness. They knew what tradition was, but they wanted to find something new and interesting—in life, in music, in poetry, in dance. How good, how just it is that Tchaikovsky, along with Pushkin and Stravinsky, was a Petersburger.

Tchaikovsky, early 1860s

FOUR

The Man

CHAIKOVSKY the man and Tchaikovsky the musician are one and the same, as far as I'm concerned. They cannot be separated. Tchaikovsky thought about music all the time. But of course, he was an extremely polite man and never let his guests know: Look, I'm busy, leave me alone. He was an attentive and caring host, like a true Petersburger; he liked to sit with them at dinner, then play Mozart four hands or listen to someone read aloud.

I don't quite understand how they examine the life and the works separately. Tchaikovsky's life is interesting only because it is the life of a great musician. One must speak of his life in terms of his music, and when one examines the music, one must remember what Tchaikovsky's life was like.

Tchaikovsky wrote to Grand Duke Konstantin that he "literally cannot live without working." He explained that as soon as he finished a composition and wanted to enjoy a rest,

73

Grand Duke Konstantin Romanov

he was immediately visited by "depression, boredom, thoughts of the vanity of earthly life, fear of the future, fruitless regret over the irretrievable past, tormenting questions about the meaning of life." In order to get away from these depressing thoughts, Tchaikovsky had to immediately embark on a new composition. And then Tchaikovsky would work for real: "I am created so that if I begin something, I cannot rest until I finish."

That's right! Once you start work, you can't interrupt it. When you make soup, you bring it to a boil right away, you don't

The Petersburg Conservatory; statue honoring Glinka on right.

heat it up a little, cool it off, then heat it a bit and cool it again. You won't get anywhere like that.

> *Perhaps that's why Tchaikovsky couldn't stand holidays. "On weekdays you work on a schedule," he wrote, "and everything goes smoothly, like machinery; on holidays the pen falls from your hands, you want to be with people close to you, to relax with them. You feel orphaned and alone."*

On holidays you feel so lonely, so abandoned. On weekdays everything goes by schedule, people work, go here and there,

76   the stores are open, everyone's fine. When it's a holiday, you
get the feeling that you've suddenly been transported somewhere else, as if you're in a movie: something alien, unfamiliar
is happening, and you're watching from the outside. You don't
even want to participate in it.

It's much harder for me to live on holidays. There's no
one on the street. The few passersby are dressed unusually;
and it's not clear where they're going. Tchaikovsky's percep-
tion is absolutely accurate! And then on weekdays it's easy to
live again.

> *You can't say that Tchaikovsky immersed himself in work
> simply to forget his troubles, to distract himself from living.
> Music for him is also a radiant and joyous force. Nadezhda
> von Meck once compared music with intoxication. Tchai-
> kovsky firmly disagreed: "It seems false to me. A person
> turns to wine in order to deceive himself, to obtain the illu-
> sion of happiness. And he pays a dear price for that decep-
> tion! The reaction can be horrible. Wine brings only
> momentary forgetting of grief and despair. And is this the
> effect of music? It is not a deception, it is a revelation. . . . It
> enlightens and brings joy."*

Music, according to Tchaikovsky, reconciles us to life forever,
while alcohol does it only temporarily. And yet Tchaikovsky
loved a good wine, loved lively, sweet champagne, just as he
loved a good cognac. He could drink a lot of it. In moments of
despair the artist has a right to a drink. And for us despair is a
normal state. The artist drinks and—ah!—it seems to him that
something good is about to happen. And his depression dis-
appears. It may return later, but the first moment after a drink
is marvelous! Tchaikovsky does not call for an end to alcohol.
He says, as I see it, that music can intoxicate much more

strongly than the best champagne. And in that, Tchaikovsky is   77
absolutely right.

> *Tchaikovsky seems to be made up of contradictions. He does*
> *not like to travel but is constantly on the road; he is always*
> *seeking solitude but is often out in society; he hates publicity*
> *and promotion of his music, but he works hard to make it*
> *popular and even becomes a conductor with that aim. Tchai-*
> *kovsky often changed his mind about his own works. For in-*
> *stance, he first said that the Fifth Symphony "came out well";*
> *after the first few performances, he "came to the conclusion*
> *that the symphony is not a success," complaining that the last*
> *movement is "horribly disgusting" to him. But finally he*
> *came to like the symphony again.*

I understand Tchaikovsky in that very well; it's not a sign of
weak character or uncertainty in your talent. It's something
else. When I finish a ballet, honest to God, I can't say whether
it works or not. On the one hand, if I hadn't liked it, I wouldn't
have finished it. On the other . . . You see, in art it's rare that
something pleases or displeases you totally, from beginning to
end. You evaluate a work in parts, in pieces. For example, you
start something that you like, you continue it, and it turns into
something else. This you like less, but you go on. Suddenly
you don't like it at all; you think, ah! this is not very good, why
did I do it? But you finish it anyway, and then it's good again.
So you've finished the work and what can you say—do you
like it or not?

> *This is particularly typical of Tchaikovsky because he*
> *usually cared not so much about the musical material itself*
> *as its development. Glazunov once told him, "Pyotr Ilyich,*
> *you are a god, since you create everything out of nothing."*

78   Even when Tchaikovsky borrows a melody from another composer, it comes out so naturally! In his opera *Iolanta* one of the main themes is a song by Anton Rubinstein. And this made Rimsky-Korsakov very unhappy! But I think, if you like something of someone else's, why not take it? The important thing is that it seem natural and fit in. Then you yourself forget that you borrowed it. And you're pleased—I did it so well! That happens when you have to meet a deadline and you're working fast.

> *Tchaikovsky always worried what the critics would say about a new work. He followed reviews closely and complained: "In Russia there is not a single reviewer who writes about me with warmth and amity. In Europe they say my music 'stinks'!!!" Hermann Laroche, Tchaikovsky's friend, recalled, "The hostility of the lowest scribbler could deeply upset Tchaikovsky."*

The critics did not understand him, and even if they praised him, they did it stupidly. That often happens: they praise you but for the wrong thing. I, for one, do not like stupid praise. They say, it's a work of genius, genius, but they don't say what it is about it that's good.

But it's nice sometimes if a person likes what you yourself like about your work. You think, Well, that's good, someone else noticed!

> *Even though Tchaikovsky was always at work, he berated himself for laziness: "I have strength and ability—but I am suffering from a disease called Oblomovism. If I do not overcome this disease, I may easily perish." And Tchaikovsky goes on to say that he is afraid of his "lack of character," that his "laziness will take its toll."*

We read Ivan Goncharov's novel, *Oblomov*, in school. [Its hero, a Russian landowner, lies on his couch and does nothing. Oblomovism is a widespread term in Russia.] There's a bit of Oblomov in us all. I sometimes think about my life that it's nothing but Oblomovism! I've done so little. Look how much Tchaikovsky accomplished! But I also think that what Russians call Oblomovism is not simply laziness or an unwillingness to work. There is also a rejection of excessive bustle, a conscious decision not to participate in the rat race for the phantoms of fame and success. Here in the West, people run all the time—hurry, hurry, like squirrels in a wheel. It looks like movement, but where are the results? The Russian says, "I will not participate in your vanity fair, I think I'll lie down on the couch and take a rest." Actually, you can think of quite a few interesting things on the couch. That's the Oriental side of Russians.

> *Even though Tchaikovsky's seeming indecisiveness made many think that he was a gentle and amenable person, he rarely retreated when it came to his compositions. A good example of this is related by Tchaikovsky himself. He played his just-composed First Piano Concerto for Nikolai Rubinstein, the famous pianist and director of the Moscow Conservatory, where Tchaikovsky taught composition. Tchaikovsky wanted a few suggestions on making the piano solo more flashy, but, he wrote, an unpleasant surprise awaited him. "It turned out that my concerto was no good; that it was impossible to play; that passages were trite, clumsy, and so unpianistic that they could not be fixed; that as a composition it was bad and vulgar; that I stole this here and that there; and that there were only two or three pages that could be left and the rest had to be either thrown away or totally redone."*
>
> *Tchaikovsky's professional pride was deeply wounded.*

"One might have thought that I was a maniac, an untal-
ented and unknowledgeable scribbler who had come to a fa-
mous musician to throw my claptrap at him." At first,
Tchaikovsky, in his words, "could say nothing from agita-
tion and anger," but when he did speak, his reply to Rubin-
stein was determined and brief: "I will not change a single
note!"

Tchaikovsky was absolutely right in his reply! Performers think much too highly of themselves. And more important, they're wrong more often than they're right. They say, "This music is no good! We won't play it!" Then some time passes, and it turns out that the audience likes this "no good" music. Then the performers begin playing it more and more often. And they forget that they had ever criticized it. Nikolai Rubinstein later played that Tchaikovsky concerto many times and very successfully—the very one he had criticized so ruthlessly at first hearing. Tchaikovsky knew his talent's worth. He even said once, "My greatest fault is my consuming pride." I understand what a colossal motivation pride can be, the desire to be better than your rival, especially when you're young. I remember when I was staging my first ballet numbers, I very much wanted to come up with something special, so that everyone would say, "Yes, this is better than Boris Romanov! More interesting than Kasyan Goleizovsky!" That rivalry existed, it did.

Tchaikovsky is capable of speaking of his music with sober
professionalism: "I want, I desire, I love people to be in-
terested in my music, to praise and love it. . . . I want my

Tchaikovsky with the young Prince Argutinsky, later an influential member of
Diaghilev's circle

82

name to be a label, *distinguishing my wares from others, and for that label to be valued, to have a market and fame." But Tchaikovsky can also pour out his raptures and despairs like a dyed-in-the-wool romantic. He weeps often. On a guest tour in New York, he could have a heart-to-heart talk with an unknown Russian woman, suddenly burst into tears, and run out of the room. Tchaikovsky weeps as he listens to music and composes it; he weeps alone, pacing his hotel room. In his diary Tchaikovsky admits that this happens to him regularly: "As it always is after a weeping fit, old crybaby"— Tchaikovsky calls himself that—"slept like the dead and awoke refreshed, but with a new supply of tears which flow ceaselessly."*

As a child I must have cried, but I don't remember exactly. I do remember that Diaghilev used to cry. In our theater men cry. That's all right. I myself would sob bitterly if someone dear to me died. Basically I'm one of those who hold in their tears, don't let them out. Sometimes now I think, well, something important is going on; it's going well, and suddenly—you have to die, be put in the grave. And I feel like weeping, but I still don't cry. Because I am responsible for the theater, for other people. Tchaikovsky was not accountable for others, so he could relax and cry. After all, men are no stronger than women, they merely pretend to be. Actually, men should cry more frequently and harder than women. Because they are bigger than women. And their secretions that make tears are bigger. Men tolerate pain or unhappiness worse than women: misfortune bends a woman—and it breaks a man.

Tchaikovsky appreciated the comfort and convenience of city life. But he could also exclaim, "Ah, the Russian country- side, the Russian spring!! That is the ultimate of everything I love." He was an avid mushroom hunter, he enjoyed his

flower garden: "The closer you move to old age, the stronger
you feel the pleasure that comes from proximity to nature."

For Tchaikovsky, life in the country was first and fore-
most an opportunity to have solitude: "I am in some sort of
exalted and blissful spiritual state, wandering around in the
woods during the day, through the boundless steppe at eve-
ning, and at night sitting by the open window and listening
to the solemn silence."

I like living in the country. When I was small, we lived in the
country year-round in Lounatiokki, in Finland. My father
built a house there. It was fun. Our house was right in the
woods, our nearest neighbors were far away. Mother loved
flowers and grew them, and we helped. We had lots of seed-
lings in small pots. I remember pansies. I love roses and carnations, too. But I guess I like roses more. Carnations have a
more astringent scent. Of course, I know very little about gar-
dening myself. I have a small house here, too. It needs to be
put in order, but I don't have time. I don't have a wife—there's
no one to run it. There are very nice people, they're ready to
help, to do everything. But I don't like having things done for
me. I'm independent, that's the Georgian blood in me.

One of the major shocks in Tchaikovsky's life was his unsuc-
cessful marriage when he was thirty-seven. In his letters to
von Meck and to his brothers, Tchaikovsky described how it
happened. He got a love letter from Antonina Milyukova, a
former student at the Moscow Conservatory; Tchaikovsky
not only responded, but he met with her. As Tchaikovsky re-
lates it: "I went to see my future spouse, told her frankly that
I did not love her but would be her loyal and grateful friend;
I described my character in detail—irritable, intemperate,
with hermitlike tendencies. Then I asked her, did she wish to
be my wife? The response, naturally, was affirmative. . . . I

84   *decided that you cannot avoid your fate and that there was*
     something fatal in my meeting with this young woman. Let
     be what will be." But according to Tchaikovsky, as soon as
     the marriage ceremony was over, his wife was abhorrent to
     him: "It seemed to me that I, or at least the best, even the
     only good part of myself, i.e., my musicality, had perished
     irretrievably. My future appeared as a pathetic existence
     and the most unbearable, oppressive comedy. To pretend for
     your whole life is the greatest suffering. How could I think of
     my work? I fell into a deep despair. I began hoping passion-
     ately for death."

I always felt that the major reason in Tchaikovsky's breakup
with his wife was his fear that he would stop composing,
would lose his musical gift. If not for that, Tchaikovsky might
have continued living with that woman, keeping up appear-
ances. But not only did he not feel any attraction for her, he
had nothing to talk to her about. That woman did not know a
single note of Tchaikovsky's compositions.

Incidentally, that can happen in any marriage. The first
time I got married, I was young, I didn't care in the least. Married . . . so we're married. Then we both went abroad. And
there, you look around, and there are so many marvelous
women. And my wife [Tamara Geva or Zheverzheyeva] began
moving away from our life, our Russian life. She spoke French
and German, you know. She kept wanting to go somewhere,
see something, do something. I sensed that she had developed
new interests. And then I thought, time to end all this.

When a few years later Tchaikovsky learned that his brother
Anatoly was getting married, he wrote to him: "There is a
certain need for tenderness and care that can be satisfied only
by a woman. I am sometimes overwhelmed by mad desire to
be caressed by a woman's hand. Once in a while when I see

pleasant faces of women (incidentally, not young) I feel it would be so good to put my head in their lap and kiss their hands."

I can understand that there can be such an impulsive desire. But I've never experienced anything like that. I have wonderful relations with women; with my ex-wives, too. We get together, talk, laugh. There was never any distance between us. But what Tchaikovsky describes has never happened to me.

One of the most famous and "romantic" episodes in Tchaikovsky's life was his fourteen-year correspondence with the wealthy widow Nadezhda von Meck. She paid Tchaikovsky a monthly subsidy, which the composer accepted gratefully, but at her request they never met (except by chance) and did not converse. When Nadezhda von Meck suddenly stopped helping Tchaikovsky in 1890 (one version has it that she learned of his homosexuality), it came as a serious blow for the composer.

Von Meck was a rich woman, and, of course, she loved Tchaikovsky. She loved him both as a composer, and, probably, as a man whom she knew well from his letters. She supported Tchaikovsky at a difficult time in his life. That was very nice of her. Von Meck, of course, was an extraordinary woman; her kind is hard to find in our day. When I was in Russia, I did not know any. But later, when I was with Diaghilev, it was not easy to meet women like that, either. Diaghilev never gave any parties, he merely went when he was invited. And then, for example, the famous and rich Coco Chanel gives a big party: we're all invited, tons of people. And it is impossible to tell who is who: all the women are fashionably dressed, *comme il faut*, but which ones are rich—you couldn't tell. Tchaikovsky

Nadezhda von Meck,
1880

OPPOSITE:
Tchaikovsky, 1866

didn't make friends with von Meck at a party, either, but through their letters.

Tchaikovsky probably felt more comfortable in the company of men, especially as he grew older. It's hard to talk to young women when you're not so young, when you're over fifty. If they're seventeen, they want seventeen-year-old friends. Of course, you can be philosophical about it: what is, is, what will be, will be. But it can still annoy you, especially if you don't want simply to make a nice impression but are seriously attracted. If you're simply in the company of several young girls, then of course it doesn't matter. Well, what do they care? Not much . . . But if you're interested in one of them a lot, that can hurt deeply. Love is a very important thing in a man's life, especially toward the end. More important than art.

88   When you're getting old, it seems that art can wait, but a
woman won't. In art, you think you understand a thing or two
already. But with a woman, that's not the case, you can't understand her totally—never, ever. Maybe she likes someone
else, and you might even be stealing her away. And you think,
That's not necessary! And it's all so confused, so complicated. . . . Horrible!

     I think that Tchaikovsky felt comfortable and good with
young men. Women immediately started making claims on
him. His ex-wife wrote letters to him all her life, hounding
him. There are people who take things like that calmly, who
don't care. But Tchaikovsky couldn't do that. With men, probably, he could be friends and even love them, and they did not
demand exclusivity. Tchaikovsky did not want to belong to
anyone exclusively, one hundred percent, because he was
afraid he would stop composing then. Music was the most important thing in his life. He wanted to be alone with his music.
That was difficult. They said that Tchaikovsky was a mis-
anthrope, because he tried so hard to avoid people. He was
tormented by the need to keep up social conversation with
wealthy ladies. They were all such time-wasters! All that nonsense about the weather, the gossip about some famous tenor
. . . or soprano . . . And every other word is "beautiful, beautiful." It's torture! And you have to bow and smile. To get
away from such horrible conversations, Tchaikovsky sometimes claimed that he was not he. That he simply resembled
the composer Tchaikovsky. He preferred having a drink with
his servant to appearing in society.

     *Tchaikovsky's Western biographers often stress the affection
     with which he treated his servants and even the servants of
     his friends. Sometimes they draw the conclusion that these
     servants were part of Tchaikovsky's homosexual circle. Per-
     haps that is so; it is hard to maintain anything with cer-*

*tainty since there is no documented proof. But it seems that in
Russia relations with servants were traditionally on a different emotional level than is customary in the West. Therefore,
Tchaikovsky could be expressing nothing more than the typical Russian "enlightened* barin *[master]" attitude toward
his servant when he writes about him in his diary: "Such a
wonderful personality. Lord! And there are people who
wrinkle their noses at lackeys because they are* lackeys.
*Why, I don't know anyone whose soul is purer or more
noble. . . ."*

People in Russia always liked their servants. That's why I'm
not surprised that Tchaikovsky wrote affectionate letters to his
servant. Here, in the West, people treat their servants much
more coldly. And Orientals don't even speak to their servants.
If a servant says anything to an Oriental master, he listens, but
does not look, does not react, sometimes he may move a fin-
ger. Or like this—with his eyes—and that's it! In the States
you sometimes see people treating their pets better than their
servants.

Incidentally, I know Tchaikovsky liked cats and dogs, but
at home he had only one dog, which he taught to do various
tricks. The Stravinskys, when they lived in California, had two
cats, Vaska and Pancho. Vaska was the favorite, and he managed to make them get rid of the other cat. Vaska did not want
to share Stravinsky with anyone. I had a cat, Murka, a good
cat. I taught her all kinds of tricks. I've always liked cats. A cat
is a lovely person, she understands everything, but doesn't
like a lot of people around, doesn't like being bothered or
upset. When you're left alone with a cat, she's wonderful! I
think cats are less servile and toadying than dogs. They're independent and proud. A beautiful woman is like a cat and like
a horse. When beautiful women run or walk, they resemble
fine horses. And when they go to sleep, they resemble cats.

90   Now I like to go watch horses at the races. In my youth, though, in Petersburg, I didn't go to the races. You had to hire a carriage to get to the horse track, and I didn't have the money for it, much less for betting. Tchaikovsky was a gambler: he liked the races, he liked playing cards for money. In Petersburg they enjoyed gambling. It's a cold windy city, and gambling warms the blood. In his opera *Queen of Spades*, Tchaikovsky wrote incredible music for the card game scene. Stravinsky, also a gambler, wrote a whole ballet called *Jeu de cartes*, in which the dancers portray cards in a poker game. I did this ballet on the stage of the Met.

> *Tchaikovsky seemed always unhappy with where he was. He returns from an exhausting trip and notes in astonishment: "Instead of joy and peace at being undisturbed by anything, I feel a vague unhappiness, dissatisfaction, even depression. . . . I have work, the weather is ideal, I've always liked solitude and always sought it, and yet with all that I feel if not miserable, then sad and in anticipation of something." At moments like that in the country Tchaikovsky loved so much, he is irritated even by trifles: for instance, that there's no one to play cards with.*

Oh, I understand Tchaikovsky so well: When you're with people, you want to be alone, you think it'll be better; and when you're alone, you're engulfed by sadness. Horrible sadness! I don't know what causes it. You'd think, you're surrounded by your family, people you've wanted to see for a long time. And then you see that they don't exist. Sometimes you start having imaginary conversations with them. And you feel that they hear and respond. But you can't tell other people about it.

Before, when I was young, I used to call my friends in moments of despair. We didn't go out to restaurants, I did the

cooking myself, and not from recipes, but from memory—by the tastes and smells of my childhood. In Russia we had servants to do the cooking, and my mother was a marvelous cook. I can still remember the taste of those dishes! And, of course, I remember what I tasted, smelled, ate everywhere. Even though I don't use recipes, I cook tasty food. My only problem is that I'm not sure about the oven, how hot it should get and how long I should keep the food in. I have to try it several times, experiment, and then decide. It's like ballet: you have to try there too—a little heat, a little cold, add a little of this, a little of that, salt or pepper. In ballet, as in culinary art, the result depends on experience, self-confidence, and intuition. And also on luck.

Tchaikovsky, who tended to introspection, admitted that sometimes he failed to see any logic in his own actions and concluded, "I think that I am doomed to a life filled with doubts and seeking a way out of contradictions." When you read his diary or letters, it can sometimes seem that, under the pressure of external events and inner impulses, the composer's personality is about to disintegrate. But every time Tchaikovsky finds the strength to overcome the crisis. His main stimulus, of course, is composing music. But what makes Tchaikovsky meet with people, seek contact with publishers, performers, to conduct his music himself—in his own words: "To put the yoke on myself"? "The answer is simple," states Tchaikovsky. "I do all this because I consider it my duty. I am needed, and as long as I am alive, I must satisfy that need."

Of course! While a composer has the strength, he must do all that! Stravinsky did it too! And it's the same thing at our theater: you have to go everywhere, give interviews, attend receptions. It's all terrible and tiring. And then you think: after all, it's for the theater, that means it's important, it's good. And then, there's something very Russian about it: "I must!" The sense of duty—that's very Russian, like in Leo Tolstoy or Dostoyevsky, the Russian feels that he is fulfilling some mission. Now, Tchaikovsky—he never was a society person, but he was a public figure and a citizen. Tchaikovsky felt that his music was needed by the people. So, as long as he was around, he tried to bring it to the people, to make it more accessible. This is what I would call a sense of duty before music. It comes from strong religious feeling. You know that it must be done, and you do it because you believe in it.

I know how faith helped reconcile Stravinsky with life. Apparently, Tchaikovsky went through the same thing. Tchaikovsky described one such occasion. Extremely upset,

he wandered around Petersburg and dropped into the Church
of Christ the Saviour to pray. The prayers, the incense, the
priest reading the Gospel—all this calmed him. Such things
happened to Tchaikovsky often.

And, of course, Tchaikovsky was a monarchist and patriot. He loved the tsar and didn't want even to hear anything
else. Tchaikovsky was not a chauvinist, but when the Russians
fought the Turks he was so worried for Russia that he couldn't
even compose. He read the papers, followed the latest political
news. He argued politics with his friends. People imagine that
composers spend all their time thinking only about music,
about beautiful things. That's nonsense, naturally. Stravinsky
and I often talked about politics, especially after a few shots of
vodka.

Pushkin, self-portrait, 1829

FIVE

Reading and Travel

READING *is one of the most blissful plea-
sures," wrote Tchaikovsky. According to him, he "gulped
down" countless books and magazines: "I read exclusively in
the evening and sometimes read late into the night. It's bad
for the eyes, but what can I do? During the day I read only
during my* repas. *I love that, even though I read somewhere
that it is not healthy."*

He loved Pushkin and Lermontov, two genius poets. For me,
Tchaikovsky is Pushkin in music: supreme craftsmanship,
exact proportions, majesty. And the music is still elegant and
dansable. Pushkin wrote best of all about the ballet. Now Lermontov, that's something else: the verse roars, everything is
vivid and emotional. Lermontov is a Russian romantic. He
lived a brief, very romantic life. Lermontov was only twenty-
six when he died in a duel.

96   *Tchaikovsky's idol was Leo Tolstoy: "I read and reread*
      Tolstoy endlessly and I consider him the greatest writer in
      the world, past and present. . . . To have him is enough to
      keep Russians from feeling ashamed when all the great things
      given to mankind by Western Europe are enumerated."
      Tchaikovsky wept over Tolstoy's works: 'The Death of Ivan
      Ilyich' is a work of tormenting genius. . . . Tolstoy never has
      villains; all his heroes are equally dear and piteous to
      him. . . . His humanity is infinitely higher and broader than
      the sentimental humanity of Dickens and almost approaches
      the view of human evil expressed by the words of Jesus
      Christ: 'They know not what they do.'"

Like Tchaikovsky, I always preferred Tolstoy to Dostoyevsky.
When Russians get together they enjoy an argument over who
is the greater genius—Pushkin or Lermontov, Tolstoy or Dostoyevsky. Tchaikovsky said that Dostoyevsky was a writer of
genius, but one he found antipathetic. He considered Tolstoy
almost a god but did not find him particularly *simpàtico* as a
man: when they met, Tolstoy said straight off that Beethoven
was a mediocrity. Tchaikovsky was astonished but said nothing. Tchaikovsky and Chekhov, on the other hand, became
close friends. They started writing an opera together after Lermontov's, but nothing came of it. I also like Chekhov; he is sad
but not sentimental. Other writers can't manage that.

And, of course, Tchaikovsky read extensively in German
and French, he knew those languages fluently. In Russia, all
well brought-up, proper people knew German and French.
Pushkin read French and so did Tolstoy. Turgenev even wrote
in French. Tchaikovsky read Schopenhauer and Spinoza in
French and Goethe's poetry in German.

Tchaikovsky loved E. T. A. Hoffmann. In Russia Hoffmann was always respected, as were other German writers,
like Goethe and Schiller. In school we studied Goethe and

Mikhail Lermontov

Schiller—in Lermontov's excellent translations. Pushkin translated French works usually; he felt an affinity for them. In general, Russia always eagerly followed the latest in the West: in literature, art, and music. The interest in the new was highest in St. Petersburg, there was a reason for calling it the "window on the West." In Moscow they cared about a good meal and a good night's sleep, they liked rich food and soft eiderdowns. In Petersburg people were lithe, unsettled, they were more ready to travel.

98

While traveling, Tchaikovsky liked to read. But he could do it only when he was calm; in moments of despair he tossed away his book. Here he is reading on a train to Berlin, but suddenly he recalls his nephew Bob Davydov: "I was so anxious to see you, to hear your voice, and it seemed such an incredible bliss that I would have given ten years of my life (and as you know, I value life dearly), to see you for just a second. The only thing I have to counter this type of depression, which you probably have never experienced and which is more horrible than anything else in the world, is drinking. And I drank an incredible amount of wine and cognac between the border and Berlin."

But of course, just what I said! Tchaikovsky liked to drink; I don't think he liked Berlin very much. . . .

Tchaikovsky wrote to his publisher: "I am echter Russe in my heart and that is probably why I find the Germans repulsive, alien, nauseating, and vile. I give them their due: I am impressed by the order and cleanliness of Berlin, I like the cheapness and availability of entertainment there, I find the Berlin Zoo excellent—and still I cannot bear German air for more than two days."

But I liked Berlin very much the first time we went there, in 1924, when we were just out of Russia. It was impossible living in Russia, it was horrible—nothing to eat, people in the West can't even understand what that means. We were hungry all the time. We dreamed of going away, anywhere, as long as we got away. To go or not to go—I never had any doubts at all. None! I never doubted, I always knew: if I ever had the chance, I'd go! We formed a small ballet troupe—Lida Ivanova, Danilova, Efimov, Tamara Zheverzheyeva, and I—and we spent a long time trying to get permission from the government to go

to Europe and show them the new Russian ballet. It was hard,
but we somehow managed to convince the commissars that it
would be good propaganda. When we reached Berlin we got a
telegram from Moscow telling us to return. We paid no attention to that telegram, as simple as that.

> *On his very first trip abroad the young Tchaikovsky headed
> for Paris; he liked the city on that trip and on subsequent
> ones: "It's good here in any season. I cannot describe how
> comfortable and pleasant this Paris is and how pleasantly a
> person who intends to have fun can spend his time. Just
> strolling along the streets and window shopping is highly en-
> tertaining. And then there are the theaters, trips to the coun-
> try, museums—everything fills up your time so that you
> don't even notice it flying by."*

Tchaikovsky had a good time in Paris because he had money.
It's nice living in Paris if you have money. But it's another
story if you're poor. After all, Paris is not a very cozy city, it's
not pleasant in every season. If the weather's bad, when it's
too cold or too hot, then it's quite unpleasant in the city. The
indigent Frenchmen, the *clochards*, complain of the cold. Of
course, if you come to Paris straight from Russia, you're not so
cold in Paris, not so scared. We Russians know how to handle
the cold. But the Frenchman feels it more.

To tell the truth, I didn't get to know Paris too well, because I was poor there. We made very little working for
Diaghilev and spent those miserable sums on food. We lived a
poor life, exactly like the one depicted in *La Bohème*. We simply didn't have the money for a good time! But we didn't regret it. First you'd feel like something strong, some liqueur or
other, and then you'd think, ah! that muck? Why not have
some tea? You'd go on thinking, no, liqueur is too strong, and
the taste is neither here nor there. While some tea would be

100   perfect! I read that in his youth, Tchaikovsky, when he ran out
of money would go to an inn in St. Petersburg, on Nevsky
Prospect, and go heavy on the tea. Tea was an inexpensive
pleasure then, just five kopeks a glass. And Stravinsky, even
though he and I had more than our share of vodka, loved tea.
Tea is a great thing, it helped keep us alive in Paris. It was fine:
we drank tea and had fun. When you don't have money in
Paris, the temptations are fewer. Monte Carlo was something
different—we had both temptation and money there, we lived
rather well there.

> *In Nice Tchaikovsky was depressed: "Naturally, there are*
> *pleasant moments, particularly in the morning under the*
> *rays of the blazing but not intolerable sun, when you sit*
> *alone by the very edge of the sea. But even these pleasant min-*
> *utes are not deprived of a melancholy cast. What then follows*
> *from all this? That old age is here, when nothing brings joy*
> *any longer. You live on memory or hope." This was written*
> *by a man who had just turned thirty-one.*

But there's nothing at all in Nice! Even the beach is boring.
You can just walk along the beach slowly, and that can be
good. But not for long, not for long. I know it—a long shore-
line, and the locals live off tourists. And when there are fewer
tourists, all the little cafés are half empty, and it's not the same
at all.

Nice is a typical resort. It's impossible to live there a long
time, even a young man will feel old there. I went to Nice to
visit Stravinsky, he had a villa there. A glorious garden, quiet,
lots of flowers. They had a rather strong scent, almost intoxicating. There were pansies, anemones, carnations. And no one
to talk to. Stravinsky was married to an old woman then, she
was even older than he. So, the Stravinsky table is set: At the

head of the table a priest, Father Nikolai, because Stravinsky 101
was very religious and he kept to that. His wife was very religious, too. This little old lady sits next to him. The children are
at the table, too, and they resemble each other terribly. Svetik
looks like Fedya and Fedya looks like his father. They're all
sitting at the table and munching some salad, then spaghetti,
and so on. All the faces are the same, and Stravinsky sees
himself in them. Do you think that's interesting—looking at
yourself all the time? I don't.

And then I always had the feeling that his wife was in his
way. Even though Stravinsky told me often that marriage was
sacred for him. He did not divorce his wife. When she died, he
married a second time. So, as I remember, life in Nice was
alien for Stravinsky, he didn't belong to it. He had nothing to
look at.

> In Rome, Tchaikovsky listened to the singing of "a young
> castrato with a marvelous voice." The experience left him
> with "an ambivalent impression: on the one hand, I could not
> help being delighted by the amazing timbre of that voice, on
> the other, the sight of a castrato elicited both pity and a cer-
> tain revulsion." Tchaikovsky did not like Rome very much,
> at least in his early trips: "All the monuments of antiquity
> and art naturally are astonishing, but as a city, Rome
> seemed gloomy, rather lifeless and boring. You can wander
> around the streets of Naples with great interest, observing
> the people and the mores. In Rome I tried wandering around,
> but I experienced nothing but boredom."

Rome, strangely enough, is not a lively city. Perhaps at one
time it was fun living there—a long time ago, centuries ago.
And now only the architecture is left. So you walk through a
ghost city which lived five hundred or a thousand years ago.

Russians were usually delighted by Venice, but not Tchai-
kovsky: "Venice is the kind of city that if I had to spend a
week here I would choke on despair on the fifth day. Every-
thing is concentrated on St. Mark's Square. Beyond that,
wherever you go, you get lost in the labyrinth of smelly alleys
leading nowhere, and until you hire a gondola and tell them
to take you somewhere, you won't know where you are.
There's no harm in traveling along the Canale Grande, for
it's full of palaces, palaces, and more palaces—all marble,
each one better than the next, but at the same time, each one
dirtier and more dilapidated than the next. It's like well-
worn scenery for Act I of Donizetti's Lucrezia.*"*

Yes, he's right! The Venice legend is created by tourists. If
people live in an ugly place and suddenly find themselves in
Italy, in Venice, it's interesting for them: you go into cathedrals, under vaulted ceilings, it's dark, statues all around. Unusual! Or the canals: you ride in a gondola and come to an
intersection. That's interesting, too. But if you live in Venice
all the time, you get used to it—so what, canals here, canals
there. The water is dirty, sometimes it stinks. For some, that
smell is Venice's greatest charm. Diaghilev, for instance, liked
the stink, he told me so.

Diaghilev and Stravinsky are buried in Venice, next to
each other. They say that Diaghilev always feared water, because a gypsy had foretold that he would die on water, and he
died in Venice, which of course is on water. But I don't believe
all these stories. Diaghilev could have died in Paris, and then
what would there be of that legend? No, it's all nonsense!

I know that Stravinsky loved Venice, he lived there all the
time. I can't imagine a better place for his grave than Venice.
Where else would he be buried—at the Russian cemetery in
Paris? Who would go there? But the cemetery on San Michele
in Venice is such a pretty little spot, and everyone goes there.

Tchaikovsky adored Vienna. And he liked Switzerland. 103

Vienna is full of life, it's a lively city! Engrossed students walk around, you can see that people are busy. It's not like Paris, where you think that everyone is on vacation. That's why even though Paris is beautiful, I don't like it. In Vienna there is a lot of serious music, and real life goes on. It's the same in Switzerland: a quiet, very sweet place, but people there aren't overly relaxed, on permanent vacation. Of course, it's nice to vacation in Switzerland, but the mountains energize you. You go out on the street, you feel like taking a walk, you head for the mountains. And you feel good! Of course, it's no fun alone. But if you're not working, it's always boring alone.

> *Wherever Tchaikovsky traveled, he was always drawn back to Russia: "Russian landscapes are much more to my taste than all the fabled beauty of Europe." Tchaikovsky wrote that in the last year of his life, but even twenty years earlier we find in his diary, written in the Alps: "O dear homeland, you are a hundred times more beautiful and dear than these picturesque monster mountains, which, basically, are nothing more than petrified convulsions of nature." It seems that Tchaikovsky likes his own Russian mountains better; he describes rapturously his travels in the Caucasus, to Tiflis, where his other brother was a high-placed official. Tchaikovsky liked Tiflis very much, he compared it to Florence: southern climate, original architecture. Tchaikovsky notes particularly that he had visited a local Turkish bath.*

Even though I am Georgian, I was born in Petersburg; I didn't get to Tiflis until 1962, at the end of our tour of the Soviet Union. The Caucasus is full of grandeur, I appreciate that. It's not like the Swiss Alps, which are cute, with tiny restaurants, but without real majesty and terror. Not the real thing. I can't

say anything about a Turkish bath, I've never had one. When I was small, we had our own bathhouse in Finland; we built a Russian wooden *banya*, the kind they have in villages. It was terribly hot inside. I didn't like it. Little children don't like it too hot. It was a steambath, with two doors. An antechamber for undressing, then a small room that wasn't too hot, then the steamroom, where they take a bucket and pour water onto hot rocks. As soon as they started yelling, "Come on, add some steam!" I'd get out of there.

I never did get a good look at Tiflis. It was boring and musty there. The architecture of a city isn't enough—the people have to be lively, too. A city dresses up in its people! Then it glows from within. Then, people were afraid to meet with us, because we were accompanied by officials all the time. We were taken around, shown everything, but people weren't allowed to come up to us.

Tchaikovsky was delighted by America, which he visited in 1891 to conduct at the opening of Carnegie Hall. He went over on a "colossal and luxurious" ship. The adventures began right away: one of the passengers decided to commit suicide, jumped overboard, and drowned. Tchaikovsky observed his fellow travelers, immigrants from Alsace. "The immigrants don't seem downcast at all. Six whores of the lowest sort are traveling with us; they are under contract to a gentleman who is in charge of them and accompanies them. One of them is quite pretty, and my acquaintances from second class are all taking turns with her physical charms." Then Tchaikovsky got seasick, and when they docked in New York he was tormented by the customs and passport formalities.

Tchaikovsky liked New York: "A very handsome and very original city; on the main street one-story houses alternate with houses nine stories tall. . . . Central Park is marvelous. And it's amazing that people can remember quite well a time when cows used to graze there." Musicians and audiences greeted Tchaikovsky enthusiastically, and he was happy: "I'm a much more important bird here than in Europe. American life, mores, customs—it's all extremely interesting, original, and at every step I bump into things that

106   *stun me with their enormity, the colossal scale compared to*
Europe. Life is full steam here, and even though the main in-
terest is profit, *Americans are quite attentive to art. . . . I*
also like the comfort, *which they care about considerably.*
My hotel room has, as do all rooms in all hotels, both electric
and gas lighting, a bathroom with a tub and a water closet,
lots of very comfortable furniture, and apparatus for speak-
ing to the hotel office in case of need, and other comforts and
conveniences that do not exist in Europe."

Exactly! First of all, Tchaikovsky was right to note that Americans keep both business and the arts in mind. And as for
comfort—in my time, too, America was more advanced than
Europe in that regard. In America, Tchaikovsky learned what
it is to become a sensation. Letters asking for his autograph
came from all parts of the United States, and Tchaikovsky responded patiently. And he was right to do so. You have to get
used to this country, it's worth the effort.

I also came to America by boat, of course, but I didn't feel
seasick—not then or any other time. Dancers should not get
seasick. If I have a choice now of ship, train, or plane, I'll take
a plane, it's faster. I remember we had problems with the port
authorities, too, something wrong with our papers. They
didn't want to let us into America. And I didn't know English.
(Tchaikovsky didn't know English too well, either, incidentally.) We even thought that we'd have to go back to Europe.
But Lincoln Kirstein took care of everything, fortunately.

I remember the smells of the harbor, the port life. I liked
New York immediately: the people are cheerful, the buildings
tall. I can understand Tchaikovsky's shock. In St. Petersburg
the tallest building was then only seven stories. I liked
America better than Europe. First of all, compared to America,
Europe is small. Secondly, everything was over for me in Paris,
there was no work. And I didn't like the people there; it was all

the same thing, over and over. And it was impossible to get
work in England. I wanted to go to America, I thought it would
be more interesting there, something would happen, something different. I would find some new, improbable friends.
Russians always want to see America. We read about cowboys
and Indians in our childhood. I read Mayne Reid's *Headless
Horseman,* and Cooper's *Last of the Mohicans.* We boys liked to
play Indian. Chekhov has a story of how some schoolboys
plan to run away to America and what happens. Then, of
course, there were American movies: William Hart, Douglas
Fairbanks, who leapt dashingly from a bridge onto a moving
train or fearlessly climbed a rope over a chasm. Life in
America, I thought, would be fun. And I was right.

Portrait of Glinka, 1845

SIX

Predecessors
and Contemporaries

T CHAIKOVSKY worshiped Mozart. People say how can
that be? They're so different, Tchaikovsky and Mozart. But
you don't have to resemble the composer or writer you like.
You can be the complete opposite—like Glinka and Stravinsky, for example. They say that Glinka's music is simple
and that Stravinsky's is difficult. Yet it was Glinka's classical
simplicity that Stravinsky loved. And Stravinsky tried to write
his opera *Mavra* as simply as Glinka had written *A Life for the
Tsar.*

> *Tchaikovsky once mused: "Perhaps it is precisely because as
> a man of my time I am broken, morally ill, that I so like to
> seek solace and consolation in Mozart's music, which for the
> most part serves as an expression of life's joys, experienced by
> a healthy, complete nature* uncorroded by reflection."

110 Now, of course, musicologists say that Mozart was not so simple and joyous, that maybe he had a confused life. But I think that Mozart knew how to be happy. He liked to sit with friends, to play his works for them: "Here, listen to what I just wrote!" And after playing, he could easily weep; he knew that he did not have long to live. Perhaps that's why he tried to enjoy every moment.

When a composer performs his own work he must experience a special feeling: "I did this, I did it myself!" Mozart could imagine an entire symphony at once in his mind! All the melodies to be written down, all the chords! Tchaikovsky envied such a gift of God, and so do I. I can't assemble ballets from beginning to end in my mind, I have to try them out. Sometimes, as I listen to music, I begin to think. There, I think, the music is going into that key, that means something like this can happen here and something like that there.... And then I think, no, I can't do that. I think maybe I'm not right for it at all. But I still have to do something, because the public is waiting for something new, some premiere this month. And you do it.

> *Tchaikovsky comments on Glinka's memoirs: "The author of the memoirs appears to be a kind and sweet man, but a shallow one, a nonentity, run-of-the-mill. I am tormented sometimes by how such a colossal creative force could coexist with such a human mediocrity and how, after a long time as a colorless dilettante, Glinka could in just one step become the equal (yes, the equal!) of Mozart, Beethoven, and whomever else."*

Tchaikovsky thought that Glinka was terribly lazy, that he could have written a lot more had he been disciplined. I don't agree. Glinka wrote lots of music. He wrote without rushing,

effortlessly. He was considered lazy for those days, when   111
Rimsky-Korsakov wrote an opera every year. Glinka wrote
only two operas—*A Life for the Tsar* and *Ruslan and Lyudmila.* I
know *Ruslan* by heart. I danced in the production of this opera
at the Maryinsky Theater. The Soviets changed the title of
A Life for the Tsar to *Ivan Susanin.* I've only now come to see
what a divine work this is; when I was younger I preferred
Ruslan. Glinka has a lot of excellent music which is not often
played now. We [New York City Ballet] danced Glinka's *Valse
Fantasie* and dances from *Ruslan. Ruslan* is in the true Imperial
style. You can see the influence of Italian music and Beethoven. I staged this opera in Hamburg. Diaghilev also knew *Ruslan* by heart and complained that they did not understand
Glinka in the West. Diaghilev told me that he once read this in
a French newspaper: "Glinka would not be bad at all if he did
not borrow his melodies from Tchaikovsky." Glinka died before Tchaikovsky had started composing seriously! Critics are
so stupid!

My father, the Georgian composer Meliton Antonovich
Balanchivadze, loved Glinka and paid for the first complete
edition of Glinka's letters. This was in St. Petersburg. I was
very young then. They even called Father "the Georgian
Glinka." He became rich when he won a hundred thousand
rubles in the state lottery. When he bought the ticket, it didn't
even occur to him to check it, but Mama looked and said, "I
think it's the right number!" And she kept after Father to go to
the state bank: "Go and tell them it's yours." Father didn't
want to go, he was too embarrassed. He finally went and told
them at the bank, "Would you please look, here, they say I
have the right number." And they said, "Of course it is! Why
didn't you come in sooner? You've won a hundred thousand!"
And they immediately gave him a check for a hundred thousand rubles.

112   Mama said to my father, "Now, we'll have money for the children's future." But Father spent it all instantly, gave it all to friends. He helped them open all those Georgian restaurants in Petersburg. Then he wanted to invest in a big project, a factory. And that's where he was lost: the expenses were enormous, they inported special machinery from the West which wasn't available in Russia. Of course, he was surrounded by crooks. Tchaikovsky's father also went bankrupt: he gave his money to a confidence woman who promised him mountains of gold. But things were even worse for my father; for his debts, he spent two years in Kresty, the famous Petersburg prison. All those Georgians kept telling him, "They can't put you in jail!" And when the investigation began, they all gave evidence against him: that's him, he's the one. And so my father was put in jail. But now he's respected in Georgia, they play his music. My younger brother, Andrei Balanchivadze, who lives in Georgia, is also a composer.

>*Tchaikovsky was as critical of Mussorgsky (whose feelings about Tchaikovsky were mutual) as he was enamored of Glinka: "I have studied Boris Godunov thoroughly. . . . I send Mussorgsky's music to hell from the bottom of my heart; this is the most vulgar and base parody of music."*

Mussorgsky has written some attractive music, but much of it is not interesting. You sometimes think, why don't I listen to some Mussorgsky? And then they play it, and it's not fascinating. But I respect Mussorgsky. Now Tchaikovsky, too—he respected Wagner but was bored by his operas. He said that you can't spend four hours listening to an endless symphony instead of an opera. But it's always interesting to listen to *The Magic Flute*. I love *The Magic Flute* best of all of Mozart's operas.

Tchaikovsky was one of the first to appreciate Georges Bizet's
Carmen: "What a marvelous subject for an opera! I can't
play the last scene without tears—on the one hand, the re-
joicing of the people and the crude merriment of the crowd
watching the bullfight; on the other, the horrible tragedy and
death of the two main characters, who were brought together
by cruel fate, fatum, and led through suffering to an inevita-
ble end. I am convinced that in ten years or so Carmen will
be the most popular opera in the world." Tchaikovsky wrote
that in 1880.

Carmen is never boring! I love *Carmen* very much, very! They
tried to make that music fit into ballet many times, but it
didn't work. *Carmen*'s story has to be told, if people are to understand it. You have to speak in *Carmen:* "I think this and
that." That's fine in opera, but you can't talk in ballet!

A long time ago, in St. Petersburg, I saw a very interesting
ballet set to music by Bizet, not *Carmen*, but his *L'Arlésienne*. It
was choreographed by Boris Romanov, whom everyone called
"Bobisha." It was danced by Romanov's wife, Elena Smirnova,
a gorgeous woman. Back then I had a crush on her. She was
twenty years older than I, I was still a kid. I hung around
backstage at the Maryinsky, watching her play the gypsy over
whom two Spaniards fight to the death. Bobisha Romanov
made it a very erotic thing—for those times. But he did not
pretend that it was *Carmen*. It was simply a flashy, very entertaining miniature, like the ones that later were presented by
Kasyan Goleizovsky.

I'm not against story in ballet, it all depends on how it's
done. Petipa took subjects that were easy to turn into dance.
But what they sing in *Carmen* cannot be translated into dance.
No one would understand anything.

Schumann is very good for dance. If you speak of com-

*Elena Smirnova, second from right, next to her husband, "Bobisha" Romanov,
in Swan Lake at the Maryinsky*

posers who were important to Tchaikovsky, you shouldn't 115
forget Schumann. He was loved and respected in Russia. Here
they don't know Schumann, he's not performed very much.
You say Schumann, and everyone makes a sour face. Now,
Chopin is played a lot here. But Tchaikovsky was antipathetic
to Chopin. Someone once tried to convince Tchaikovsky that
his music resembled Chopin. He grimaced and said, "Perhaps." People don't leave a composer alone, they keep trying
to find whom he resembles, and it's all wrong. Chopin is diamonds, ornamentation, *parure*. Tchaikovsky and Schumann
are substance.

SEVEN

"But the Music Is So Noble!"

T CHAIKOVSKY wrote only six symphonies. Haydn wrote a hundred. Of course, Haydn was a great master. But also in the old days symphonies were not so hard to write. Those symphonies all sound the same. A million symphonies—and they're all fine, everything's right in them! Sometimes you hear them on the radio; it's a pleasure, but you can predict every turn ahead of time. You surely can't do this in Tchaikovsky's symphonies!

They say that Tchaikovsky is great at nothing but wonderful melodies. That's not true! He intertwines his melodies in complex ways, he practically builds Gothic cathedrals out of them, harmonizing inventively, bringing them through different tonalities in a masterful way.

Balanchine working on stage on Adagio Lamentoso, *from Tchaikovsky's Sixth Symphony, at the 1981 New York City Ballet Tchaikovsky Festival*   117

118
*Tchaikovsky wrote that he never composed "abstractly"—
that is, when a musical idea came into his head, he already
knew what instrument would play it. "I invent a musical
thought at the same time as its instrumentation."*

He's incredible at it! And no one speaks of it, or even understands it. In the old days this is what they did: they wrote
music and then arranged it; it was arranging, not orchestrating.
Tchaikovsky's orchestration is like silver, because he invented
music just the way it would sound. For instance, the clarinet in
the middle of the Andante in the Fifth Symphony—it's divine.
When Tchaikovsky wrote symphonies, he *thought* orchestrally.
He uses wind instruments wonderfully: in the Second Symphony the flutes move toward each other, they seem to flicker;
in the first movement of the Fifth Symphony there is a brass
chord—trumpets and trombones—that is like an explosion!
Just like the horns in *Queen of Spades* when the old countess
dies. It's genius! Or the sad waltz in the Fifth Symphony—two
gloomy-sounding clarinets accompanied by French horns,
which create the impression of ominous, angry jangling.

It's difficult to read Tchaikovsky's scores, because the
keys keep changing. Prokofiev's scores are simple, because all
the instruments are in C. But in the old days all the instruments were made to be played in different keys. When you
look at a Tchaikovsky score you have to keep transposing, it's
a lot of trouble. Even our conductor Robert Irving—who
knows everything and can sight-read on the piano brilliantly—even he looks and says, "What's this!" Of course,
great musicians do better at this than we do. But once you
learn what is in which key, and sweat over it a bit, you'll understand it all.

Tchaikovsky's First Symphony is very balletic, it's subtly
written, like a watercolor. The waltz is especially appealing.
Too bad that the Second and Third symphonies are rarely

played. In my day there was a joke at the Petersburg Conservatory: a student is asked how many symphonies Tchaikovsky
wrote, and he replies, "Three—the Fourth, Fifth, and Sixth."
The Second has a brilliant finale, and the Third, another of
Tchaikovsky's marvelous waltzes, a whole ballet scene exquisitely orchestrated.

Tchaikovsky called his First Symphony Winter Dreams;
*once he came upon a painting of a winter road and said that
it "could be an illustration" of the first movement. He wrote
a long letter to von Meck about the "programme" of the
Fourth Symphony: it includes the "everyday sea," recollections of his youth, and a picture of a folk holiday. Tchaikovsky's famous sentence in his notebook—"Should I throw
myself into the arms of Faith?"—is related to his Fifth Symphony.*

That's all nonsense! Tchaikovsky composed music first and
then came up with titles. Titles are important for publishers,
they say you have to call it something, it will sell better. They
called one of Haydn's symphonies the *Drum Roll* so that all
those ladies in Philadelphia—small feathers in their hats, five
o'clock tea and all that—could say, "Oh! the *Drum Roll* Symphony!—we must go hear it!" They come, listen to it; in the
second movement the kettledrums go "boom!" and that's it,
you can sleep to the end of the piece. There's another Haydn
symphony, they gave it the stupid title *The Clock*. There's a
staccato rhythm in it going clam-clam-clam-clam-clam. And
everyone goes home happy, they've heard a clock run. Haydn
hadn't thought about a clock at all!

Tchaikovsky didn't name his *Pathétique* Symphony, either;
it was his brother's suggestion, and Tchaikovsky accepted it.
He cried a lot as he composed it. He wrote that this symphony
was his Requiem. In the first movement you can hear anticipa-

Manuscript page from the Pathétique *Symphony*

tion, fear, and then the Orthodox funeral chant appears; in the second, a strange waltz in five-four time; in the third, a sound like scurrying mice, as in *The Nutcracker*. And in the finale, it's all over; the trombones and tuba play the chorale. And it's all masterfully, wonderfully connected: the melodies in the finale resemble the theme in the first movement. And the tonalities are similar. Everything, everything is thought out! It's extraordinarily interesting to follow how it's all done. I want to stage the last movement of the Sixth: I don't know yet how it will look, but there won't be any dancing. Simply a procession, a ritual.

Evgeny Mravinsky

I thought of doing it this way. We have old costumes from some operas: dark red, burgundy, and black with long golden sleeves. There will be twenty or thirty people dressed in these strange hooded gowns, with gold faces. And in the middle of the last movement of the Sixth, when the major begins, suddenly the sun appears, or something like that. And I'll have angels—white, with enormous wings and golden hair. And maybe they'll hold lilies. I want to send out girls with garlands, I want them to come out with the angels. But I haven't decided whether their hair will be up or down.

I like the way Evgeny Mravinsky conducts the Sixth. We

122 knew each other back in Petersburg; he was studying at the conservatory and so was I. We kept running into each other at the Maryinsky Theater. He was an extra and later worked as a pianist at the school. Later he became a famous conductor, but that was after I left Russia. Mravinsky has been with his Leningrad Philharmonic about as long as I've been with our theater. He's younger than I am and resembles me, but he's taller. He used to write poetry. I didn't understand too much poetry back then. And here was someone who looked like a clever person, and a poet to boot. So, I thought, why shouldn't I set his poetry to music? And I did. Mravinsky also conducts Tchaikovsky's Fifth Symphony well. He shows not only the melodies, in his performance you can see the polyphony—it's all complicated, interwoven, but you can hear it crystal clear. The Fifth Symphony is one of my favorites.

> *The critic Hermann Laroche, who was called the composer's "first and most influential friend" by Tchaikovsky's brother Modest, wrote this about Tchaikovsky: "I rarely met an artist who was as difficult to define by a single formula. . . . Can one say that he was a 'purely Russian soul'? Tchaikovsky combined in a very complicated way a cosmopolitan responsiveness and ability to absorb everything with a strong national-Russian underpinning." Tchaikovsky argued against separating Russian music from European; in one letter he compares European music with an orchard in which different trees grow: French, German, Italian, Russian, Polish, and so on.*

Tchaikovsky was a European from Russia, that must be understood. It was difficult for him: after all, he was Russian, he wanted to remain true to Russian music but at the same time not to fall behind Europe. He was accused during his lifetime of not using folk music enough. But he has folk music themes

in the Second, Fourth, and Sixth symphonies, and in the ballets, everywhere. Tchaikovsky does not want to sound nation-
alistic, but he still remains Russian. Rimsky-Korsakov keeps
wanting to show how Russian he is, but his music sounds like
Wagner, more German than Russian.

Tchaikovsky and Stravinsky are similar: Stravinsky did
not try to write especially Russian music, either, but when you
listen to him now you hear that it's Russian, of course. And
not only *Firebird*, or *Petrouchka*, or *Les Noces*. Take *L'Histoire du
soldat:* the soldier is a Russian soldier, he plays the violin. A
French soldier would have played the trumpet. I recently listened to *Perséphone* again—there's so much Russian music in it!
And in Stravinsky's small pieces, say his pieces for piano four
hands, you hear Russian things all the time.

> *Laroche wrote about Tchaikovsky: "His works form a sort of
> middle line between Gounod and Schumann: they have bril-
> liance and at the same time inner warmth, they please the ig-
> noramus and the connoisseur, they can become fashion's
> objects and they can outlive its whims." Laroche also recalled
> that Tchaikovsky "feared sentimentality in music, did not
> like excessive rubato in piano playing, and laughed at the ex-
> pression 'play with soul.'"*

Tchaikovsky wrote a lot of gentle lyric music, but there are
also stormy passages, almost Dostoyevskian. Russians have it
all. But in Tchaikovsky it's in harmony, it's all proportional.
You can study at length how he did it, what tricks of the trade
he used. And people say—soul! I don't understand what that
is—soul in music. Tchaikovsky was right to laugh at it. When
people like something, they say it's *dushevno*, soulful. They
confuse two completely different words—*dushevnyi*, "soulful,"
and *dukhovnyi*, "spiritual." Tchaikovsky's music isn't soulful,
it's spiritual.

126   Emotions in Tchaikovsky's music are misunderstood, too. People think emotions are something petty: You go out with a girl, eat, drink, your digestion is working well. Or on the contrary, you have a corn, your shoe is tight, and you want to cry. But those aren't emotions at all! Tchaikovsky has all the emotions—joy and sorrow—expressed through music, they're down on paper. Tchaikovsky's emotions are all in the elegance of the musical line, in the architecture of his music. You can tell easily what you like in your everyday life—that is, the petty things—but you can't tell about music. Music contains profound feelings and emotions; people are born and die with them, but they can't explain them. It's like Lermontov's line "What do we care whether you suffered or not? . . ." Perhaps your wife has died, but you're composing a joyous piece because it's been commissioned and you have to fill the order. And it may come out to be a great work. That's what it means to express emotion in music. Of course Tchaikovsky knew what his music was about, but that cannot be put into words. What are Tchaikovsky's orchestral suites about? I don't know. The first movement of his Second Suite is called *Jeu des sons.* What does that mean? Maybe Tchaikovsky imagined something concrete in the other movements, maybe he pictured something? We don't know that, we simply listen to the wonderful music.

The first movement of the First Suite is sheer genius, it's complete in itself. We used to dance the march from that suite in Russia in the ballet *The Fairy Doll,* conducted by old Drigo. The Third Suite is a masterpiece. Think of that waltz: gloomy, almost grim, but not in the least sentimental! And that waltz is orchestrated masterfully; it starts in the violas, then goes to the lower register of the flutes. You can't stop listening closely. The last movement of the Third Suite, Theme and Variations, is now played rather frequently. The theme is so elegant and restrained—sheer Mozart!

Tchaikovsky's pieces based on Shakespeare are incompa- rable: *Romeo and Juliet, The Tempest, Hamlet*. Shakespeare suited him. After all, *Hamlet*, for instance, isn't all philosophy or something, it's also a real play for the theater with bloodshed and all kinds of spectacles invented just for the audience. Shakespeare's *Midsummer Night's Dream* is very entertaining. I know it by heart, in Russian, of course, because I was in a production in Petersburg when I was young. I acted and danced.

Tchaikovsky wrote about Bellini's and Gounod's operas based on Romeo and Juliet: *"In them Shakespeare is mutilated and distorted beyond recognition. . . ."*

He also changed Shakespeare around, as it suited him. Tchaikovsky made a short thing from *Romeo and Juliet*. That's hard, to make something short. You are reading Shakespeare: where do you start, where do you stop? It's an enormous play. Tchaikovsky doesn't retell the plot. In his Shakespearean music everything is proportionate, and still there is inner tension. They say that's romanticism. But I think, no, it's not romanticism. But neither is it academism, as in Rimsky-Korsakov. It's an Imperial style.

Some people think that Tchaikovsky is a simple composer. Let them listen to his *Mozartiana* suite. There's much to think about: why did Tchaikovsky decide to arrange Mozart? We know that he adored Mozart. And Mozart was not often played in those days. Tchaikovsky said that he would orchestrate some small Mozart keyboard works, and then they would be performed more often. But that's not the only thing to understand. Tchaikovsky took Mozart's prayer *Ave Verum*. Why? Probably we'll never know. It became more than an arrangement, it's a stylization—like, for instance, the way Stravinsky later reworked Pergolesi. It is Tchaikovsky's homage to Mozart, homage of a Russian composer to an Austrian. It's to-

Suzanne Farrell and Ib Andersen in Mozartiana

tally modern music, especially the Variations and the Gigue. Incredible harmonies! Tchaikovsky was not yet old when he wrote *Mozartiana.* Had he lived a long life, I cannot even imagine what he might have achieved. *Mozartiana* probably gave an impetus to the whole idea of modern stylization. I hear a strong Petersburg note in it. And I like the fact that Tchaikovsky wrote *Mozartiana* in Georgia.

The Serenade *for strings was, Tchaikovsky admitted, his "favorite child." In his concerts he performed it more often than his other works. Its first movement is also created like an homage to Mozart; in it, wrote Tchaikovsky, "I paid tribute to Mozart; it is a conscious imitation of his manner,*

Serenade, *New York City Ballet*

*and I would be happy if it were found that I was not too far
from my model."*

I knew and loved Tchaikovsky's *Serenade* ever since I was a
child. I always wanted to stage it. And it turned out to be my
first ballet in America. I hadn't planned it, it just happened
that way. I just wanted to do the *Serenade,* so I did. Besides, we
didn't have a real orchestra then, only a small one. And *Serenade* could be played by a small group. After we did *Serenade* it
became popular here. That happened with many of Tchaikovsky's compositions. Say, all pianists play his First Piano
Concerto. But what about the Second? The Third? Or the *Concert Fantasy* for piano and orchestra? Tchaikovsky's Second

130   Piano Concerto may not be the greatest music, but it's perfect
for dancing. After we did it, everyone started playing it. Before, no one played it at all. Now, when I turn on the radio, I
hear the Second Concerto more and more frequently. And the
same thing happened with the Third Piano Concerto and with
Tchaikovsky's suites. Before, when we played his music, people made faces: come on, what is this? Now on the radio they
try to play Tchaikovsky before we do. So we're trying to do
the same thing for Tchaikovsky that he did for the little-
known works of Mozart.

> In 1881 Tchaikovsky wrote to Nadezhda von Meck: "I
> think I've found myself an appropriate pastime. With the re-
> ligious mood that I am in, I would like to study Russian
> Church music. I began studying our ancient church chants
> and I want to try to harmonize them." Tchaikovsky wrote
> Vespers, to which he added the modest subtitle "An At-
> tempt at Harmonizing Church Music for Chorus." In an-
> other letter he described the Vespers thus: "I am not at all
> the independent artist in it but merely a transcriber of our
> ancient church chants. If I do not satisfy those who expect po-
> etic impressions from this work, then perhaps I may render a
> serious service to our church singing. . . ."

I'm not very impressed by Tchaikovsky's church music. He's
right, it's more for the actual service than for listening in a
concert hall. It was not easy for Tchaikovsky, of course: the
Orthodox Church never had its Bach. Take Bortnyansky or
Vedel—that's not interesting music, Tchaikovsky didn't like it
either. Now Stravinsky wrote marvelous music for the church.
Stravinsky's Canticum sacrum and his Requiem are great things,
but they are not for the Russian Church, they're for the Cath-
olic Church, even though Stravinsky himself was a fervent
Russian Orthodox.

The premiere of Tchaikovsky's Violin Concerto took place in Vienna, and the most influential European music critic of the time, Eduard Hanslick, wrote a review. In a letter to von Meck, Tchaikovsky summarizes it for her: "Hanslick writes that in general, as far as he knows my works, they are uneven, totally tasteless, crude, and savage. As for the Violin Concerto, the beginning is tolerable, but it gets worse as it goes on. At the end of the first movement, Hanslick says, the violin doesn't play but roars, screams, and growls. The Andante also begins well, but soon turns into a depiction of some wild Russian holiday where everyone is drunk, everyone's face is coarse and repulsive. 'A writer,' continues Hanslick, 'said of a painting that it was so realistically repulsive that it gave off a stench; listening to the music of Mr. Tchaikovsky, it occurred to me that there can also be stinking music.' A curious review, isn't it? I don't have any luck with critics."

Violinists like that concerto: a friend of mine who's a violinist told me that the second movement resembles Jewish music. I also like Tchaikovsky's *Méditation* for violin, which has another name, *Recollections of a Beloved Place.* When I listen to that music, I understand how lonely and sad Tchaikovsky sometimes was. But the music is so noble! And most important, as soon as it starts, you know that it's Tchaikovsky. Practically from the first note you can say—it's him, it's all his! Not many achieve that.

The Queen of Spades: *design by Vladimir Dmitriev, cofounder of Balanchine's Young Ballet company and a close friend.*

EIGHT

Operas

VERY time I'm asked which of Tchaikovsky's operas is better, *Eugene Onegin* or *Queen of Spades*, I reply that I can't say. I think both are extraordinary. I know them by heart, I performed in both when I was young—in the ballet scenes, of course—and I staged *Eugene Onegin* myself. Sometimes I'm asked for advice: which opera is better to produce, which will the audience like better? Then I ask in turn: what is your repertory, what did you do last year, what do you plan for next year? It's important to know your public, what it's used to, what it expects. And perhaps, I would suggest to start with *Queen of Spades*. Tchaikovsky used a novella by Pushkin which described a true Petersburg story: The young officer Hermann wants to get rich, to win at cards; for that he is prepared to do anything. He causes the old countess's death, he abandons the girl he loves. He's unlucky, he loses all his money, goes mad, and commits suicide. Cards, money—they

134 understand that here in the West. And there were officers like that here, too.

Onegin is harder to understand, the passions aren't so strong, even though there is a dueling scene. You have to think over Onegin, you have to begin by reading Pushkin's novel-in-verse Eugene Onegin. People don't like to read carefully anymore, they flip pages—hurry, hurry! All they care about is the plot. While in Onegin what's most important is the atmosphere: a provincial Russian estate, a young girl who falls in love with a visiting dandy from the capital, a duel between friends, unrequited love.

> When Tchaikovsky began writing Eugene Onegin, he wrote to his brother: "You won't believe how obsessed I am by this subject. I'm so glad to be rid of Ethiopian princesses, Pharaohs, poisonings, all sorts of stiltedness. What a treasury of poetry in Pushkin's Onegin. I am not mistaken; I know that there will not be many stage effects or movement in this opera. But the poetry, humanity, and simplicity of the plot in conjunction with the genius text will more than make up for these lacks."

Tchaikovsky even called his Onegin not an opera but "lyric scenes" after Pushkin. Onstage we see the unhurried life of the provinces, every detail lovingly drawn by Tchaikovsky. Even down to this: when the old nyanya sings, you can tell that she is from Moscow. You can hear the Moscow accent in her music! I know that because I easily distinguish the Moscow pronunciation from the Petersburg one.

But, of course, Tchaikovsky was a man of the theater; that is why the opera has the dramatic duel scene: Onegin kills his friend Lensky. I'm sometimes asked who's right and who's guilty in that duel. And I reply, I don't know what "guilty" means. This isn't a criminal trial, it's an opera. Maybe Pushkin

described a duel because duels were popular in Russia then.
He himself died in a duel, as did the other great Russian poet,
Lermontov. In my day, however, only German students fought
duels.

Or perhaps, Pushkin put his characters in a duel because
it was a good way of resolving a dramatic situation. The hero
for an author is after all only a chess piece; the author moves
him around in order to win the game. That's the way Pushkin
wrote—a page, then another page, of great poetry. And as for
who's guilty and who's not—that's not the author's business. I
remember how the great tenor Sobinov sang Lensky at the
Maryinsky Theater. After the duel scene, when Onegin kills
Lensky, many people would leave the theater, they weren't interested anymore. That's so stupid. The important thing isn't
the duel but the music. In the last act, the third, Tchaikovsky
wrote a lot of wonderful music—a polonaise, a waltz; how can
you leave without hearing them?

> *Tchaikovsky insisted, "Opera demands concision and speedy
> action." When Grand Duke Konstantin rebuked Tchai-
> kovsky because the characters in* Queen of Spades *repeated
> words and phrases, which does not happen in real life, the
> composer replied: "If necessary I am prepared to brazenly de-
> viate from realistic truth in favor of artistic truth. These two
> truths are totally different. If you carry the striving for real-
> ism in opera to its extreme, you will inexorably reach a total
> rejection of opera itself: people who sing instead of speak-
> ing—that is the height of falsehood. Of course, I do not wish
> to return to obsolete operatic conventions and nonsense, but I
> certainly have no intention of obeying the despotic theories of
> realism."*

Stupid people like to joke that in opera they sing "Let's run,
let's run," but no one leaves the stage. If they want to see peo-

Eugene Onegin: *staging at the Maryinsky Theater, 1884; at far right, Leonid Sobinov as Lensky.*

138   ple running, they should go to a stadium, not an opera house.
When someone sings "let's run" in an opera, that means that
the composer felt he needed dramatic music there. They say
that Tchaikovsky's *Eugene Onegin* and *The Queen of Spades* are
not the way Pushkin wrote them. If Tchaikovsky had wanted
to do it the way Pushkin has it, he would have had to write a
long play, everyone would speak and not sing, and so they
would resemble normal people. And then there would have
been no opera, it's as simple as that. Pushkin's *Queen of Spades*
is an entertaining story, but if the only reason someone goes to
the opera *Queen of Spades* is to find out whether the hero won
or lost at cards, he'd be better off staying home.

   The Queen of Spades is the most Petersburgian of Tchaikovsky's operas, and it was written in Florence. Written
quickly, in six weeks. And the opera develops quickly and
clearly, it reaches its peak in the fourth scene and then flies toward the denouement; this opera is masterfully constructed.
That fantastic quintet in the first scene—a surreal stop that can
occur only in opera: people stand and sing a long, long time
about how frightened they are. In the movies they would run
and leap about, but that's good only in the movies.

>   *Nazar Litrov, Tchaikovsky's brother's servant, went with
>   Tchaikovsky to Florence, and he left a curious diary of how
>   Queen of Spades was composed. "At seven in the evening
>   I came into Pyotr Ilyich's room and said, 'Time to stop.'
>   Pyotr Ilyich keeps making those squiggles! 'Just a minute,' he
>   says and then does another squiggle, hitting the keys of the
>   piano with one hand. Lately Pyotr Ilyich has been telling me
>   everything—that's understandable, because there's nobody
>   but me to tell anything. During his bath he told me how he
>   finished the opera. 'Well, Nazar,' he turned to me and began
>   telling, 'Hermann committed suicide!' Pyotr Ilyich cried all
>   that evening, his eyes were red, he was all tired out. He feels*

sorry for poor Hermann! Then Pyotr Ilyich played me the death of Hermann that he wrote and his tears began flowing again. I like those tears! If, God willing, that opera is seen and heard on stage, then probably many will shed tears, following Pyotr Ilyich's example."

Tchaikovsky wept because he liked what he had written. I guess composers can't do otherwise. Even Stravinsky, when he listened to his own music, could cry easily, especially if he was at home. Now people are amazed to hear that. They imagine that Stravinsky calculated his music like a mathematician. Actually, Stravinsky was very involved when he composed.

When Tchaikovsky had to write sad music, he imagined something sad; he said so himself. We dancers work differently—after all, we invent movements that don't exist in real life. When Tchaikovsky wrote operas or love songs, he had the words, but we don't have words. When I do a ballet I don't think about happiness or sadness, I think about the composer and his music. I can't cry over the Prodigal Son or Orpheus because they've gotten themselves into a mess. I have enough problems with the music; it's very hard to come up with movements that don't contradict the music, that suit it. And then you think, how do I do it so that in this spot the man's arms go up and call the woman. And so that it will be interesting, elegant or funny, and so on. That's our whole art! And it's difficult, you have to think a lot about it.

Sometimes I look at modern dance: the same gesture is used in a million different situations—here, and there, and somewhere else. And it's all the same. That's because they don't think enough about the gesture. Some of them, perhaps, do think, but they are insufficiently trained or insufficiently inventive. Of course, we're not always successful either, so I shouldn't brag.

So you sit and think, how do you make the movement go

140 with the musical line and not with the accents within a bar? If in the music there is a strong accent, the dance doesn't have to have one. You look, the music is in three-quarter time, but in the notes that could be six eight. And in turn, six eight isn't simply six even parts: the accent can fall on the even note or on the odd one. You have to keep all this in your mind. And so, when I'm doing a *pas de deux* to music by Tchaikovsky, I don't think about the *pas de deux* but about the music, about Tchaikovsky.

> *The majority of Tchaikovsky's operas are written on Russian subjects. In explaining this fact, Tchaikovsky wrote, "I generally avoid foreign subjects, for the only things I know and understand are Russians, the Russian girl and woman." And in another letter we find a typical statement: "I need people, not dolls. I willingly will undertake any opera, where, even if without strong and unexpected effects, creatures similar to me experience sensations that I have experienced and which I understand."*

That's the essence of it all! Tchaikovsky explained it all! Sometimes people are amazed that so much of Tchaikovsky's most marvelous music is addressed to women. And think of the female characters in his operas: Maria in *Mazeppa*, Nastasya in *The Sorceress*, *Iolanta!* Or Liza in *Queen of Spades!* The scene when Tatyana is writing the letter in *Eugene Onegin*—a work of genius, perhaps the best in the opera. They say how can it be, Tchaikovsky and women, what do they have in common? But that's not important! The feeling is important, not the object. Some like women, some like men. If you could look into a person's mind, there would be a lot hidden in there that cannot be revealed. No one discloses the whole truth about himself, and it's especially difficult for an intellectual to speak

about himself. But he can write a poem or music. And if you're   141
a genius like Tchaikovsky, it will be wonderful.

I saw Oscar Wilde's *Salome* in Russia, staged by Konstantin Mardzhanov, an unforgettable production. Salome says incredible things to John the Baptist! Could Wilde have been
thinking about a pretty boy when he was writing it? Of course!
I'm certain that he was! It doesn't matter that Salome is a
woman, that she has breasts and female hips, the essence of
the feeling is what counts.

In *Queen of Spades*, Liza has an astonishing aria when she is
waiting for Hermann. A woman can't write like that! Even if a
female poet writes to a man, it won't be with such passion. A
man wrote that! And that's the way it always was, men always
wrote and spoke of love: Pushkin, and Tchaikovsky, and Stravinsky, and all of us sinners.

Pavlovsk, 1910

NINE

Swan Lake and *The Sleeping Beauty*

T CHAIKOVSKY'S ballet music is as wonderful as his operas: you can sing it! Take any *pas de deux*—from *Swan Lake*, for instance—or any of his incredible waltzes. Their melodies are absolutely vocal. Think of the exquisite theme from the middle of the waltz at the beginning of *Swan Lake!* Or the waltz from the first act of *Sleeping Beauty*—so much charm and brilliance! Or the melody of the Lilac Fairy played divinely by the strings as the French horns give a soft background with their chords. If that were sung, it would be unforgettable! Dancing Tchaikovsky's ballets is sheer pleasure. I know, I danced in them myself. Tchaikovsky's music helps you a lot, you come out onstage and suddenly everything works, everything's easy, you're flying.

Tchaikovsky loved ballet from his childhood. Recalling the visit to Moscow of the composer Camille Saint-Saëns, who became friends with Tchaikovsky, his brother Modest wrote:

144   *"In their youth both not only adored the ballet, but did perfect imitations of the ballerinas. And once at the conservatory, wanting to show off their artistry to each other, they 'performed' the small ballet* Galatea and Pygmalion *on the conservatory stage. Saint-Saëns, 40, was Galatea and performed the role of the statue with extreme conscientiousness; Tchaikovsky, 35, took the part of Pygmalion. Nikolai Rubinstein, conservatory director, played the piano. Unfortunately, besides the three performers, no one else was present at this unique presentation."*

Tchaikovsky's friend Hermann Laroche recalled that Tchaikovsky's love of ballet was not at all typical of the Russian intelligentsia; Laroche wrote down what one of Russia's most influential and well-educated journalists said to him in 1869: "You shouldn't idealize the ballet so much. The ballet exists to arouse impotent old men." Laroche remembered Tchaikovsky's reaction: "When I tried to tell Tchaikovsky that our purists denounce the ballet as a seductive and lascivious spectacle, Tchaikovsky looked at me in astonishment: 'Ballet is the most innocent, the most moral of all the arts. If that is not so, then why do they always bring children to the ballet?'"

I agree with Tchaikovsky! But it is true, in the older days ballet was considered a lewd thing. Of course, there were balletomanes who were not interested in dancing but only in pretty dancers. During the performances they sat in the smoking room of the Maryinsky Theater and discussed the nice bodies of their favorites. And an usher would come when the mistress of Mr. So-and-so was about to do a solo. Then that gentleman would get up and go to his box to shout "Brava!"

There was almost no ballet criticism back then, either. When they wrote about the ballet, everything was reduced to sexuality: they described the dancers' beautiful necks, arms,

and legs. There was a famous critic in Petersburg, his name
was Akim Volynsky, I knew him well. He was drawn to ballerinas and created a whole ballet theory out of it: that in ballet,
eroticism is the most important thing, and so on. In his reviews
he described how big the thighs of his favorites were, things
like that. And other critics also went all out praising ballerinas'
thighs, because they were living with those ladies. They were
famous Petersburg balletomanes. They've all died now. It's
easy to laugh at them, but we won't insult them. They were
Petersburg eccentrics, originals, there's nobody like them now.

Tchaikovsky was convinced from the days of his youth
that ballet was an art, equal to the other arts. And this was a
hundred years ago! Most people are only coming to that viewpoint now. I remember that American parents used to think
that ballet school was a place of debauchery. And how does a
ballet school differ from a music school? If you're an onlooker,
you see boys dancing close to girls, and you imagine that they
spend all their time indulging lewd thoughts. Actually, when
you dance, there are no erotic impulses at all. Absolutely
none! It's out of the question, completely! Dancing is so hard,
it takes a lot of time and energy. When you start working, all
erotic feelings disappear. Of course, you can find some girl in
the corps de ballet and have an affair with her, but a real ballerina in the theater doesn't think about sex—not onstage and
not offstage.

The stage eliminates sex. You come out onstage and fly
toward her, and she reaches out to you and throws herself at
you. You're so worried, you barely see her. But you have to
catch her and support her. That's a difficult thing to do. It's
pure technique, not sex.

It may seem from the audience that the dancer onstage is
aroused by holding the ballerina's hand. That there's something lewd in it. Nothing of the sort! He's just trying to do his
job well. The man in ballet is the accompaniment to the

146 woman's dancing, he is only the second half. That's why it's called support. The man supports the woman, he doesn't carry her. It's dancing, not sex. Those two things must be separate.

Balletomanes did not understand that, and tragedies occurred as a result. In Petersburg I danced with Lida Ivanova, a gorgeous ballerina, extremely talented. She was beautiful, maybe a bit plump, but in good shape. Working with her was easy and a pleasure. I did the *Valse Triste*, to music by Sibelius, for her. Now, when I recall *Valse Triste*, I think that it probably was terrible, but at the time everyone liked it a lot. Lida Ivanova was a big hit in *Valse Triste*. It was her star turn, her hobbyhorse. Her humpbacked horse! Lida, by the way, danced Pearl in the ballet *Little Humpbacked Horse*.

I had known her since we were children, I had always liked her. I was short then. I was so short that I jokingly signed my letters *Maloross* [the term for Ukrainians who come from Little Russia, or Malorossiya; also a pun, literally meaning "grew little"], even though I was Georgian. Lida danced the *Fée aux Miettes* and the White Cat in *Sleeping Beauty*, and then the classical trio in *Swan Lake*. She was a wonderful Fairy! I danced with her in Lev Ivanov's *Magic Flute* to music by Drigo.

Lida liked to sing, and I sometimes accompanied her in Glinka's love songs. She numbered famous actors among her friends—Kachalov, from Moscow Art Theater, Mikhail Chekhov. And, of course, she had admirers who were big shots. And this led to catastrophe.

When we decided to go abroad—Zheverzheyeva, Shura Danilova, Efimov, and I—Lida Ivanova was supposed to go with us. Shortly before our departure one of Lida's admirers talked her into going for a motorboat ride on the Gulf of Finland. He was a big shot in the Cheka, the Bolshevik secret police, and he always took trouble with us, wined and dined us, spent a lot of time with us. I remember, he used to kiss Lida's

shoulders. He had an affair with her—not love, just a balletomane intrigue. It's so easy, after all!

There were five of them in the boat. A big ship crashed
into it. The motorboat split up and Lida drowned. I think it
was all a set-up. They shouldn't have collided: the ship had
time to turn. And then, Lida was a marvelous swimmer. The
case was quickly hushed up, there wasn't an investigation. I
had heard that Lida knew some big secret, and they didn't
want to let her out to the West. They wondered how to get rid
of her and, apparently, decided to fake an accident.

> *Laroche wrote in 1893: "I wouldn't call Tchaikovsky a
> dyed-in-the-wool balletomane. I've never heard him use tech-
> nical ballet vocabulary words like elevation, ballon, and so
> on. Well, actually, I learned those words from him, but
> Tchaikovsky used them only to admit that he did not know
> the subtleties of the art. However, Tchaikovsky did once tell
> me that some ballerina was doing the* pas de cheval. *I
> won't say precisely how far his knowledge of the leg construc-
> tion went; but in the aesthetic sense Tchaikovsky was always
> an admirer and proponent of the ballet. . . . He had the pro-
> foundest disgust for the philistines who attended perfor-
> mances for the sole pleasure of seeing naked dancers."*

I feel that if you are going to be fully involved with the performance, you have to know at least a bit about how it's done.
You must understand something of ballet technique. The audience will enjoy dancing more if it knows some of ballet ter-
minology. But most important of all, naturally, is to have a
good eye! If you have that, all those words aren't that important. Even without knowing what *elevation* or *ballon* is, a person
with good eye can see whether we're dancing well or not. Of

ABOVE: *Balanchine with Lida Ivanova, 1921*

OPPOSITE ABOVE: *Balanchine, center, with members of his Young Ballet company*

OPPOSITE BELOW: *Kasyan Goleizovsky*

150 course, we try to dance not just well but a hundred times better—so that even the least knowledgeable audience will see
that it's good.

Ballet is very hard work, both physically and mentally. It
demands colossal concentration. Someone once said to me
that dancers work as hard as policemen: always alert, always
tense. But you see, policemen don't have to be beautiful at the
same time! But we have to do all our tricks so that people are
pleased, so that the public thinks, there, that's classical art.
And the dancer meanwhile is standing there tensely, won-
dering how to keep supporting the ballerina. The arm is simultaneously hard and soft. He leads and places the ballerina,
his body follows his arm. You have to know how to do all that!
And look good while doing it!

And then, in our theater it is important that the dance not
be at variance with the music. Other theaters don't give a fig
about that. The dancers improvise onstage, do whatever they
feel like, and the orchestra drags on behind them, playing
slower or faster, as suits the dancers. In our theater everything
is fixed and calculated: how much time a leap will take, up,
down—exactly. More precisely than in operas. Singers sometimes allow themselves all kinds of indulgences, slowing down
wherever it suits them. But not with every conductor! If von
Karajan is conducting, or some other celebrity, the singers
can't sing as they like, they sing as the composer wrote it.

Our dancers work cleanly, and that's very difficult. Take
Suzanne Farrell—a clean dancer, no mistakes. A ballerina can
try hard and still not succeed. That exactness of execution—
the kind Farrell and Kyra Nichols have—is God given. Arthur
Rubinstein played the piano wonderfully, but he hit a lot of
false notes. He used to say, "If they paid me for every false
note, I'd be a millionaire!" We are not Rubinsteins, we have to
work clean. I try to explain that to the young dancers. We have
a lot of young people in our ballet, I chose them all myself. If

they work hard, they'll be trained so that they'll look decent onstage even when they're old; they'll be able to perform until they're forty.

That's not a pleasant topic, I know. But dance is for young people, you can't do anything about that. When you approach forty, it's hard to dance. Maybe in other professions forty is

152   nothing. But for us—it's being old. Ballet is like boxing. Muhammad Ali could beat everyone, but only when he was young. That's the nature of things. Horses are like that, too: three-year-olds are fine, but when they're five, it's not the same.

But who said that you must be onstage for your whole life? You should dance while you have the push. You can tell when what you've been able to do becomes too hard. That's life. In life you first do one thing and then another.

There's a famous riddle: What walks on all fours in the morning, on two legs at noon, and on three in the evening? It's man. As a child he crawls on all fours, and in the evening of his life, when he's old, he uses a cane. We dancers are made differently, and, of course, are trained better than the average person. But even we cannot escape the laws of man and God.

They sometimes say that a young ballerina is nothing now, but later, when she matures, she'll be good. No! Take Darci Kistler—she's seventeen and she's already wonderful, you can't say a thing about her. She doesn't need to learn how to understand, she already understands. You have to begin like Darci, so that everything is ready from the start, while you're still very young. Because ballerinas are like flowers: the bud opens and that's when it's good, by the next day it's not right anymore. The next day another bud opens.

Sometimes, fading flowers have an astringent aroma. Their odor is strong, intoxicating. But that's for a special taste. Some—like Diaghilev, for instance—like the smell of fading leaves, fading flowers; others don't. It's like with cheese: some like smelly cheese, but I hate Roquefort. I like young cheese. I'm a Georgian, and they don't have smelly cheeses in the Caucasus. They eat young goat cheese. At our house in St. Petersburg the cheese was hard, we broke off pieces and poured boiling water over it. We ate it with hot pancakes, delicious. A very good cheese we have here is Italian Parmesan. You

shouldn't grate it, you should eat it, but eat it when it's   153
young—sparkling and sweaty. And dancers are good when
they're young.

Tchaikovsky, who wasn't a dancer, even he worried about
his passing youth. And what worried him more than gray hair
or wrinkles was whether he'd have the strength and health to
keep on composing. To sit and write notes is physically a very
exhausting thing, I know that personally. And Tchaikovsky
didn't simply write notes. He wept over his compositions,
spent sleepless nights. A composer must be strong. Stravinsky
understood this, so he always tried to stay in good shape, did
special exercises. He was very strong, Stravinsky, even though
short. Few people know that.

> *Laroche recalls why Tchaikovsky turned to the ballet: the
> composer wanted to test himself in a fantastical musical
> drama, to get away from opera's realistic limitations, as
> Laroche put it, into "the kingdom of dreams, whims, and
> marvels." Laroche continued, "In that magical world there
> was no room for words, it was pure fairy tale expressed by
> pantomime and dance." He pointed out, "Tchaikovsky could
> not stand realism in ballet."*

I don't even understand what that is supposed to mean—real-
ism in ballet. A story? Tchaikovsky was a wise man, and naturally he was little interested in story lines in ballet. How can
you take the story of *Swan Lake* seriously? They took a German
fairy tale and reworked it for a ballet: an evil man, Rothbart,
bewitched girls, turning them into swans. It's time for a young
prince to marry, he falls in love with a girl-swan, and naturally
nothing good comes of it. It's nonsense! I remember when
Swan Lake was performed at the Maryinsky Theater—*no one
ever understood anything!* The ballet was on all night, and half of
it was pantomime: everyone spoke with hands. We dancers

154 naturally understood everything, we were taught to use our hands to say, "From there will come a man now who will . . ." And so on. It's all taken from deaf-mutes, from their vocabulary. Dancers use many of the same signs: for house, and money, and things like that. In ballet school in Petersburg pantomime lessons were called *mimika*. We were taught *mimika* twice a week along with makeup lessons. It's a whole science. In Petersburg, I know, some balletomanes took special courses to understand what was going on onstage.

Fokine told me how the great Lev Ivanov did *The Magic Flute*. There are many mime scenes in it. Ivanov had problems with how to sign "Call the judge here." "Call" and "here" were easy. But how do you sign "judge"? And he decided to show scales with his hands, because of the "scales of justice"! That's ridiculous! If you seriously present that onstage now, the audience will laugh, they'll be bored. Because all that is incomprehensible to the public now. And who needs it?

I don't want to get rid of pantomime completely. There is some pantomime in our theater, too—for instance, in *Harlequinade*. But it must be understood that it was long ago, when everything else was different. Porcelain was made differently, and people traveled differently—in carriages. In our day pantomime was a useful thing, because you needed something to move along the action, to shuffle the characters so that everything came together at the end. But many things age in art. Take the cinema: I remember seeing *The Cabinet of Dr. Caligari* in my youth; it was very interesting! I saw it again recently; it's nonsense, totally incomprehensible. I didn't like comedy films too much. But I do remember Max Linder—he was funny, I could watch him. And not so long ago they played Max Linder—and no, he's not funny, he's boring. When I went to Hollywood the first time in 1937—I did various things for Sam Goldwyn there—I liked it, it was fun! But if you were to see those films now, they'd probably look nonsensical, stupid. If I

Marius Petipa

were suddenly summoned to Hollywood now, probably everything would be different, I would have to reinvent everything some other way. Westerns are the only films that I liked before and still like now. Maybe because there is nothing superfluous in them. Simple things without pretentions—they don't age as quickly. You watch a Western and think, ah! there's *something* to this. . . .

In ballet you must strive for things to be simple, so that the audience understands what's going on. But you must remember, what was understandable yesterday is no longer understandable today. When Petipa did *Esmeralda*, everyone

156 knew what *Notre Dame de Paris* was. And they didn't have to show it—everyone understood. But now you have to show everything and explain everything, and that's not ballet anymore. Tchaikovsky used to say "going to the ballet for the plot is like going to the opera for the recitatives."

> *Tchaikovsky wrote: "The procedure for composing ballet music is as follows. A subject is chosen, then the theater management develops—in accordance with its financial abilities—the libretto, then the ballet master compiles a detailed plan of the scenes and dances. And it gives in detail not only the rhythm and character of the music, but the actual number of bars. Only then does the composer begin to write the music."*

Of course! That's exactly how we worked with Stravinsky. When a composer is doing a ballet, it's more important for him to know the number of bars needed for a particular scene than the plot. When I went to see Stravinsky in California, where he was living, to work on *Orpheus*, we sat down together and discussed each moment of the ballet. And I would say, "I need a *pas de deux* here." Stravinsky would ask, "How long?" I would reply, "A minute or two." Stravinsky would get angry and say, "That's nonsense. I must know exactly. If it's a minute, that's one kind of music, if two, it will be something entirely different. Maybe it will be a minute and thirty seconds?"

Orpheus was my idea, mine and Lincoln Kirstein's. Of course it was up to me—if I was a true professional—to give Stravinsky a precise assignment. Otherwise a composer can't work. Now critics argue whether the end of Tchaikovsky's *Swan Lake* should be happy or tragic, love conquers death or death conquers love. I don't understand any of that. It's all nonsense. And I'm certain that Tchaikovsky didn't care. He was given an assignment: we need so much music here, now we need a

Balanchine's teacher Andrianov as Siegfried in Swan Lake

transition, then an Adagio. So he used his old music. For instance, Tchaikovsky took the Adagio of Odette and Siegfried in *Swan Lake* from his early opera *Undine*. He destroyed *Undine*, but he put the duet from it in *Swan Lake*. Tchaikovsky did not throw away good music.

> *Tchaikovsky enjoyed the rehearsals of* Swan Lake, *which began at the Bolshoi Theater. He wrote to his brother: "If*

158   *you only knew how funny it is to watch the ballet master
composing dances to the sound of one violin with the most
profound and inspired air. It made me envious to look at the
dancers, smiling at the imagined audience and relishing the
opportunity to jump and whirl, fulfilling their 'sacred duty'
as they did so."* Tchaikovsky participated in the production;
the designer of Swan Lake *recalled the composer's special interest in the final scene: "On Tchaikovsky's insistence we
made a real whirlwind—twigs and branches broke on the
trees, fell into the water, and were carried away. This scene
was very effective and amused Pyotr Ilyich."* However, this
was Laroche's review of the premiere of Swan Lake *on the
stage of the Bolshoi in 1877: "I can say that I've never seen a
more meager ballet in my life. The costumes, sets, and machinery did not make up for the mediocrity of the dancing.
No balletomane could find five minutes' pleasure in it. But
what a delight it was for melomaniacs."*

Raving about the music, Laroche wrote, *"Swan Lake
has no message, it contains only such-and-such amount of
beautiful music. Perhaps, it was the very paucity of the plot
that so inspired Tchaikovsky."*

They did not understand *Swan Lake* at the Bolshoi, and they
made it into a flop. Later they wanted to perform some of the
ballet for the tsar, and Tchaikovsky's publisher asked the
composer which act he thought was best musically. Tchaikovsky replied, "The second." After Tchaikovsky's death, Lev
Ivanov restaged the second act, and then Marius Petipa himself joined him, and they did the whole ballet at the
Maryinsky. It was a great success! They didn't know how to
stage *Swan Lake* in Moscow, they ruined Tchaikovsky's music,
but the Petersburg people gave it its due.

I put on *Swan Lake* here, trying to preserve Ivanov's main
ideas. I'm a Petersburger, after all! Of course, I added a few

things, changing or adding a little, but basically it's all his, Ivanov's.

Lev Ivanov was, they say, an extravagant man of the Petersburg type. He drank a lot, died before Petipa, even though he was much younger. I did not know Ivanov, but I understand that he was a great man. I danced in his *Magic Flute.*

We try not to drag out *Swan Lake*, so that Tchaikovsky's music sounds in all its beauty. Presently in Russia and Europe *Swan Lake* barely moves, as if the dancers are afraid of spilling. For instance, the Danse russe: you're supposed to feel a real Russian push in that. And instead a few ladies fall asleep on their feet onstage. That's wrong.

When Tchaikovsky's ballet Sleeping Beauty *was done in 1890 in St. Petersburg in Marius Petipa's staging, the public adored it; people say that in those days Petersburgers greeted each other not with "Hello" but with "Have you seen* Sleeping Beauty?" *The newspapers, as usual, mocked Tchaikovsky: "His music can be called* tactless," *wrote one, making a pun on the Russian word,* takt, *which is both tact and musical measure. The reporter of* Peterburgskaya gazeta *went on: "This is a fairy tale for children and little old people who have fallen into second childhood.... But there is no ballet as we understand it! In the audience, the music was called either a 'symphony' or a 'melancholy'."* Critics *wrote that* Sleeping Beauty *was a stupid mix of Russian and French.*

People have forgotten that classical ballet is not a Russian art but actually French or Italian. Like fencing, for instance. Of course, there may be Russian fencing champions, but that doesn't mean anything. Look at how dancers are dressed—all that came from France and Italy. And our vocabulary is French. It is true that Russians learned this craft extremely

160   well, but that was because the emperor spent enormous sums on the ballet and imported the best teachers from Europe. But I don't think that ballet is specifically Russian.

Of course, there are ballets, like *Little Humpbacked Horse*, where the story is Russian, the dancers appear in Russian costumes and do Russian dances. There are other ballets with Russian dances as well. But if, say, a Georgian ensemble comes over from Russia, they dance Georgian dances, not Russian ones. Ukrainians bring Ukrainian dances. But we don't say that dancing is Ukrainian or Georgian art. It's the same for classical ballet; it flourished in Russia because it was under the protection of the tsar and the court, but that doesn't mean that classical ballet is a Russian art. Especially now, when they're afraid of pure ballet in Russia.

Plain dancing, without a story, is not approved in Russia now; it's given the strange name "formalism." When our ballet went to Russia in 1962, I saw that they were afraid of what we were doing. Reporters came and asked, "Why do you show things like this? You can't do that! Ballet isn't just dancing! There has to be a story!" They had to have a story. Without a story, they think it's not good. "There must be a plot!" What plot? What plot is there in *Swan Lake?* Well, a prince comes out with a feather in his hat, and that's the plot.

They say, "We agree with *Swan Lake*—that's a classic." They can't bring out Russian *muzhiks* onto the stage or show the revolution in *Swan Lake*. But their new ballets all have plots. They even have a ballet about the Chinese: There's this wealthy Chinese, a terrible man, and he exploits other Chinese, who are poor. Russian sailors come and rescue the oppressed Chinese. And suddenly they break into dance! The composer Glière wrote nightmarish music for this ballet. His Russians dance to the song "Little Apple." He stole that song, it existed before him. It's music from Odessa. We had chansonniers from Odessa come to Petersburg and sing. I remem-

ber there was one called Mikhail Savoyarov; he sang
interesting Odessa songs: "Alyosha, sha, take it half a tone
lower. . . ." Or "Bubliki": "And in the rainy night, take pity on
me, a miserable peddler. . . ." And that famous "Apple" was
also from Odessa. That song was very popular right after the
revolution, we all sang it: "Hey, little apple, where are you
rolling? If you land in the Cheka, you won't come back!" The
Cheka, Soviet prison! And Glière turned that into a revolutionary dance.

> *Fyodor Lopukhov, considered one of the greatest experts in*
> *Russia on the choreography of Petipa, wrote that "in com-*
> *paring* Swan Lake *with* Sleeping Beauty *a split opinion*
> *arises—as to which of these masterpieces of choreography*
> *should be awarded the first prize. I prefer* Sleeping
> *Beauty," Lopukhov decided.*

I agree with Lopukhov completely. *Sleeping Beauty* comes first
and only then *Swan Lake. Sleeping Beauty's* libretto is perfect for
the ballet, written by Petipa himself and Vsevolozhsky, director of the Imperial Theaters. Vsevolozhsky wanted to resemble a Frenchman, he was an elegant gentleman, he collected
porcelain and other objets d'art. Vsevolozhsky was very good
to Tchaikovsky. It was through his efforts that Emperor
Alexander III granted Tchaikovsky a lifetime pension of three
thousand rubles annually. For *Sleeping Beauty* Vsevolozhsky
chose a French fairy tale by Perrault: The wicked fairy Carabosse makes Princess Aurora fall asleep, and Prince Desiré,
with the help of another fairy, a good one, brings her back to
life. Everything ends with a wedding.

The plot, when you get down to it, isn't important in
Sleeping Beauty either—it's Petipa's dances that are. Lopukhov
is one hundred percent right: *Sleeping Beauty* is a pure diamond.
Lopukhov was a wise man, he was the first to come up with a

Fyodor Lopukhov

"Dance Symphony." I learned from him. Lopukhov took Beethoven's Fourth Symphony and staged the ballet *The Grandeur of the Universe* to it. Lopukhov said you can't throw silly plots at symphonic music, it won't work. It didn't work for Isadora Duncan. Even Fokine didn't come out too well when he took Rimsky-Korsakov's *Schéhérazade* and Liszt's *Préludes*. You have to manage without plot, without scenery and opulent costumes. The dancer's body is his or her main instrument, and it must be visible. Instead of scenery, change the lighting. Lopukhov used to say, "Forward toward Petipa!"

Photo after the 1890 premiere of The Sleeping Beauty

That is, dance expresses everything with the help only of music. That was the essence of Lopukhov's now-famous "Dance Symphony." We all participated in it, Lopukhov did it with us. We were all young and happy. The old ones didn't want to be in Lopukhov's production. No one did! And so we came to him. He was so pleased. Lopukhov was a good musician, he played the guitar very well. His sister, a ballerina, married John Maynard Keynes, the economist.

The critic Volynsky attacked us all, because we got in the way of his being a great ballet patron. Lopukhov headed the

164   ballet troupe of the Maryinsky Theater, and Volynsky wanted
       to unseat him. Volynsky blasted me, attacked Lopukhov for
       his *Grandeur of the Universe.* It's hard to work when you have no
       one to talk things over with. I recently heard how Misha Mik-
       hailov described my early number *Valse Triste* to music by Si-
       belius. He describes it correctly. I did it especially for Lida
       Ivanova. I remember I was very pleased with the way Lida
       performed it. And then you begin to think, maybe it only
       seems to have come out well? Maybe it's all wrong? Who can
       you talk to about it?
            Now Tchaikovsky, he consulted often with Laroche.
       When young Tchaikovsky was severely criticized for his grad-
       uation composition at the conservatory, Laroche wrote him a
       letter: "You are a great talent, the hope of Russian music."
       This may sound funny, one young man telling another that
       he's a genius, but it's so encouraging when you're in doubt
       and no one, but no one, wants to help! And Tchaikovsky, in-
       cidentally, did not remain in his friend's debt. He convinced
       Laroche to become a critic. And as Laroche was lazy, Tchai-
       kovsky wrote down Laroche's articles for him as he dictated
       them! And so he helped Laroche become a famous Russian
       music critic.
            Naturally, we had smart people in Petersburg—say, the
       artist Volodya Dmitriev, with whom I did Toller's play *Poor
       Eugen* at the Theater of Academic Drama [formerly Alexan-
       drinsky Theater]. Dmitriev wanted to be an actor, he studied
       with the great Vsevolod Meyerhold himself. Nowadays many
       people forget that Meyerhold was famous even before the rev-
       olution; he worked in the Imperial Theaters, directed operas
       at the Maryinsky. I was in his production of Gluck's *Orfeo.*
       The ballet part of it was Fokine's. The idea was for the audi-
       ence not to be able to tell where, onstage, the corps de ballet
       was and where the opera chorus was; one was supposed to

ABOVE: *Laroche, left, with composer Alexander Glazunov, 1892*
RIGHT: *Vladimir Dmitriev*

blend into the other. It was very interesting, the production was received very well. Later I participated in rehearsals for Stravinsky's opera *The Nightingale*, which Meyerhold was getting ready at the Maryinsky Theater. It was also remarkable. It was completely the reverse of *Orfeo*. In *Orfeo* the impression was that everyone was both dancing and singing, while in *The Nightingale* the soloists sang from scores, sitting on a

166   bench, a lively pantomime unfolding around them. No one noticed Meyerhold's innovations in *Nightingale*, because by then no one had time for the theater: it was right after the Bolshevik uprising, there was nothing to eat. But I learned the music well, and so later, when Diaghilev asked me to stage Stravinsky's ballet *Le chant du rossignol*, I was able to do it quickly.

Dmitriev was scrawny, like me. His father was a Soviet bigshot, and so Meyerhold, who shouted at all of us, was careful with Dmitriev and took him on as a designer. In one play Dmitriev had a piano suspended from the sky. No one knew why it was there, but Meyerhold liked it.

Another artist I remember is Yakulov—they called him Georges, too. Dmitriev was a very secretive and taciturn man. Yakulov, on the contrary, liked to party and brag. He drank a lot, smoked a lot, loved women. Dmitriev, they say, became a famous theater designer under Stalin. Yakulov died young and everyone has forgotten him, but he was a marvelous artist. He did Prokofiev's ballet *Le Pas d'Acier* for Diaghilev, and it excited *tout Paris* because they waved a red flag around onstage. It was always interesting to talk with Yakulov.

We were also helped by the artist Boris Erbstein and the critic Yuri Slonimsky. Slonimsky even took private dance lessons from me to better understand the ballet. There was one more intelligent person we could consult with, that was Ivan Sollertinsky. He was interested in both music and ballet. Sollertinsky was a temperamental orator. He hurried to say as many words as possible in the shortest time; he gasped, stuttered, and lisped all at once, and all you heard was "pshh-pshh-pshh." So it was fascinating to listen to him.

Sollertinsky never tried to convince—he simply stated his point of view. And it was of no significance whatever whether you agreed with him or not. Sollertinsky liked Lopukhov's

"Dance Symphony." He also liked my ideas on the ballet. He   167
knew some twenty languages, I think. Once Sollertinsky
showed me his notebook: all the notations were in old Portu-
guese so that no one could understand.

They were great minds, and the conversation usually
went on until morning. We discussed lots of interesting
things, but what came of it? We had no money, there was no
time—we had nothing. And that's what came of it—nothing.
Well, maybe something.

We called ourselves the Young Ballet. It was then that I
did a big *pas de deux* for Shura Danilova to music from *Sleeping
Beauty*. I danced in it with her. I had invented that *pas de deux*
earlier, back when I was in school. It came about like this: I
was looking at the old score of *Sleeping Beauty* in the
Maryinsky. The numbers are not shown consecutively, by
plot, but it's simply tons of music. And I was looking and
suddenly saw that the violin solo in the second act was sheer
genius! Incredible music from beginning to end. A big thing—
five or seven minutes, I think. Tchaikovsky composed that
solo for Leopold Auer, the famous violinist, a soloist in the Imperial Theater; Auer later taught Yascha Heifetz and Nathan
Milstein. But they just threw that music out at the Maryinsky,
they never played it. Petipa died, and no one else understood
why such a long violin solo was necessary. Lopukhov used to
say that it was Nikolai Sergeyev, the chief *régisseur* of the ballet
at the Maryinsky, who threw it out because, you see, there was
still another entr'acte, enough music to shift scenery.

Lopukhov always complained a lot about Sergeyev, he
called him incompetent. I don't think that Sergeyev was incompetent, he was simply uninteresting. If I do *Sleeping Beauty*,
that entr'acte will definitely be in it. It's incredible music, it
should be played in concerts. I even suggested it to Nathan
Milstein.

168   There's lots of music in *Sleeping Beauty*, whole huge can-
vases of it. Tchaikovsky may not even have wanted to write it
all, but Petipa demanded it from him. He wrote to Tchaikovsky along these lines: I need music for the coda—lively,
ninety-six measures. Or: bird song, twenty-four measures. Or
he demanded "general animation from eight to sixteen measures" from Tchaikovsky, or some variations. And so Tchaikovsky added, wrote in, threw out. Tchaikovsky didn't even
orchestrate some of the numbers, they were written simply for
piano.

In *Sleeping Beauty* there is the so-called apotheosis at the
end, to the music of the anthem "Vive Henri Quatre." It's an
old French song, very beautiful. Before the apotheosis, Tchaikovsky had written a mazurka, because Petipa had asked him
to write music with a great lift to it, so that they would all leap
around. Then Petipa demanded that Tchaikovsky write another galop. But the galop was not too good, so they didn't put
it on at the Maryinsky and simply moved from the mazurka to
the apotheosis. When Diaghilev produced *Sleeping Beauty* in
London in 1921, he commissioned Stravinsky to orchestrate a
few numbers. And Diaghilev reinserted that galop. But it's
better without it.

Princess Aurora and Prince Desiré are considered the
main characters of *Sleeping Beauty*, but actually the wicked fairy
Carabosse gets the most attention. The character dancer
Alexander Chekrygin was excellent in the part at the
Maryinsky. I enjoyed watching him from the wings: his cape
danced with him, like a partner. I would like to do the complete *Sleeping Beauty* sometime. I agree with Lopukhov that it is
the best of the old ballets, second only to *Giselle*. Petipa was a
wizard, he was the first ballet master to realize that Pyotr Ilyich
Tchaikovsky was a genius. That wasn't so easy: the composer
was still around, the public didn't like him, the critics didn't
like him. But Petipa surmised it, and he guessed that because

the music of *Sleeping Beauty* was so lush and brilliant he should 169
build his choreography on movements *en dehors*. It isn't so
simple to find your own approach to Tchaikovsky. Petipa
created "the Tchaikovsky style" in ballet.

No one knows anymore how to do *Sleeping Beauty* the right
way. All over the world ballet companies do it horribly, because they don't understand it at all. In Russia at the
Maryinsky Theater, *Sleeping Beauty* was done magnificently.
The curtain went up, onstage there were lots of people, all
dressed in opulent costumes by Konstantin Korovin; in our
day dancers were dressed well, even we children were cos-
tumed beautifully. The waltz with garlands was begun by
thirty-two couples, then, as Petipa conceived it, sixteen pairs
of children would appear. The men lined up in corridors, and
we children danced inside these moving corridors, while the
dancers held the garlands over us. Then the men left the stage.
They carried the garlands, the ladies followed, and after them
came we children with baskets in our hands. The audiences
went wild.

When they prepared the premiere of *Sleeping Beauty* at the
Maryinsky, they spent fifty thousand rubles on the costumes
alone—an enormous sum! And what stage effects and magical
tricks! It was a grand *féerie*. *Sleeping Beauty* must be an extravagant spectacle. A lot depends on theater management in a case
like that. In Russia, if I were in favor there, I could do it well,
they wouldn't stint on this. But here, no one understands
Tchaikovsky. It's music of such nobility! But they don't care.
Because they don't know a thing about French or German
fairy tales or about Russian music. Whatever you do is good
enough for them. And if you do it better, they won't even understand that it's better. . . .

Petipa's *Sleeping Beauty* was sheer genius. But, of course, if
I do *Sleeping Beauty* it won't be a simple repetition of what Petipa did. I will have a somewhat different approach, I will de-

Costume designs for The Sleeping Beauty *by Konstantin Korovin, 1914*

velop my own ideas. I'll see what of Petipa's dances suits our day and what doesn't. So probably I'll have to make additions, cuts, things like that. Ballet isn't a museum, where a painting can hang for a hundred or two hundred years. And even a painting needs to be cleaned once in a while. If it cracks, they

restore it. But every museum has rooms where people don't stop, they just look in and say, "Ah, it's boring in here, let's go on." Ballet can't survive like that. If people are bored at the ballet, they'll stop buying tickets. And the theater will simply disappear.

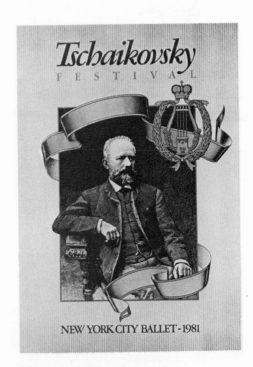

LEFT: *Balanchine in the wings at the 1981 Tchaikovsky Festival of the New York City Ballet*
RIGHT: *Festival poster*
BELOW: *Balanchine in Leningrad in 1972, with former school friends*

Scene from the 1892 premiere of The Nutcracker

TEN

The Nutcracker

FOR a lot of people, Tchaikovsky is *The Nutcracker*, but not the ballet in full, only the suite from it. But, of course, the whole ballet must be heard and seen the way Tchaikovsky intended it to be. *The Nutcracker* is Tchaikovsky's masterpiece. He said beforehand that he would write music that would make everyone weep! I danced in *The Nutcracker* as a child at the Maryinsky Theater. It was considered Lev Ivanov's staging, but actually Petipa had thought it all up himself. Petipa grew ill or suddenly got scared—who knows what might have happened—and the production appeared under Ivanov's name. Still, *The Nutcracker* was Petipa's idea, certainly. I danced various parts in it: I was the Mouse King, and the Prince, and later I did Bouffon's dance with the hoop in the last act.

    The Nutcracker is a story by E. T. A. Hoffmann that was incredibly popular in Russia. Tchaikovsky loved it. But Petipa

Lev Ivanov

did not develop the plot from the Hoffmann story, he took the version by Dumas *père*. Later, when the score was being published, there even were problems about whether Dumas' estate should be paid a royalty. But Tchaikovsky wrote to the publisher: not a word about Dumas, keep it under your hat. Petipa was French, he could relate better to the French fairy tale. He never did learn how to speak Russian well. People say that when Petipa tried to speak Russian, he came up with all kinds of inadvertent obscenities. But you don't need to know Russian for the ballet, all the vocabulary is French, so the dancers had no problems understanding Petipa.

Mikhail Fokine

*Hermann Laroche wrote in a review of Tchaikovsky's ballet:
"Say what you will against children's fairy tales, you cannot
deny that we fell in love with them as children and that they
have become part of our psyche. You cannot deny that fairy
tales contain some of the profoundest ideas that concern man-
kind. And it is a fact that in our eyes so-called children's
stories are becoming more and more stories for adults, re-
vealing their profound significance."*

Hoffmann's *Nutcracker* is a serious thing wrapped into a fairy
tale. The girl Marie gets a Christmas present, a toy nutcracker.

178   At night she learns that the Nutcracker is a bewitched prince, on whom the Mouse King has declared war. Marie saves the Nutcracker from the mice. The grateful Nutcracker brings her to the kingdom of toys and sweets and then marries her. Of course Hoffmann does not make it all so simple—Marie may have dreamed the whole thing. There's a lot of irony and allusion that only adults can understand. When Hoffmann's *Nutcracker* is published for children, they do a simplified version. Dumas also simplified it, and made it more French.

Petipa, since he did not read German, got all the names wrong in his *Nutcracker*. The Christmas party in Hoffmann is at the home of Dr. Stahlbaum, while in Petipa he is President Silberhaus. Petipa calls the girl Clara, while in Hoffmann Clara is the name of Marie's doll. In Hoffmann the place is called Konfetenburg while Petipa called it Konfituerenburg; I rather like that change. Konfituerenburg is a marvelous word! You can't even pronounce it the first time. I also like the German word *Schlaraffenland*—the land of the lazy, with rivers of milk and shores of pudding.

It's an interesting thing that the story by Dumas *père* never did catch on in Russia. There everyone knows the Hoffmann *Nutcracker*, and no one knows the one by Dumas. In Russia Hoffmann was highly revered. They love him more there than they do in Germany. The Germans don't like Hoffmann for criticizing them. Hoffmann offended everyone, he was a true Romantic. In Russia they immediately put him on a par with Shakespeare. Pushkin wrote his *Queen of Spades* under Hoffmann's influence, of course. In *Queen of Spades* it is not very clear if the old countess's ghost really appears or not. Does the ghost actually tell the secret of the three cards? Or is it all the mad officer's delirium?

The artist Alexandre Benois, who worked closely with Diaghilev, speaks of Hoffmann, Pushkin, and Tchaikovsky

together: "Pushkin's Queen of Spades *is a Hoffmanniade*   179
in the Russian style and Tchaikovsky's Queen of Spades
is a Hoffmanniade in the Petersburg style." And Benois adds
that he infected Diaghilev with this passion for Hoffmann.

You can see something of Hoffmann in Stravinsky's *Petrouchka,*whose plot Benois helped develop. There are dolls in
it, too. And they also come to life. Stravinsky told me that he
particularly liked Tchaikovsky's *Nutcracker* because there is no
heavy psychology in it, just an entertaining spectacle, understandable without tons of words. And, of course, Stravinsky
was wild about Tchaikovsky's orchestration in *The Nutcracker,*
especially, I recall, the Chinese dance. Tchaikovsky used a
small orchestra first, and then the full orchestra, but the sound
does not change, it remains spare. Stravinsky said that Tchaikovsky must have learned that from Bizet.

There's a lot of Russian music in *The Nutcracker* but also a
lot of stylized numbers. For instance, the guests dance the old
German dance *Grossvatertanz,* and the overture to the ballet resembles Tchaikovsky's beloved Mozart. The march is also
written in Mozart's spare, light style. Everything in *The Nutcracker* is exquisitely crafted. I would call it the Viennese style.
In Petersburg, we loved Viennese pastries and tortes. *The Nutcracker* is like them.

The Nutcracker is a ballet about Christmas. We used to
have a fantastic Christmas in Petersburg. Ah, how fantastic it
was! I was small. For me Christmas was something extraordinary. Naturally, Christmas is no Easter. At Easter the church
bells pealed joyously throughout the night! Nothing is like
Easter. But for Christmas St. Petersburg was all dark and
somehow strange. It wasn't the way it is now, with everyone
shouting, running around panting as if it's a fire instead of
Christmas. Back in Petersburg there was a stillness, a waiting:
Who's being born? Christ is born!

I've never seen a Christmas like we had in Petersburg anywhere else—not here in America nor in France. It's hard for us old Petersburgers! I tried to get people in the Orthodox church in New York to take Christmas more seriously, more solemnly, with understanding. But nothing came of it. They

Senate Square, St. Petersburg

get to church with their candles and it starts: ha-ha-ha, ho-ho-ho. Russian talk, gossip. It's all wrong!

In Petersburg they had the Christmas service at nearby St. Vladimir's. And naturally in all the big cathedrals: at the Kazan, at St. Isaac's. An unforgettable moment of mystery:

Cathedral of St. Isaac, St. Petersburg

when the candles were put out, the church was plunged into
darkness, and the choir came in. They sang magnificently! In
the Orthodox church, the service is a real theatrical production
with processions and all that. The priests come out in pairs
wearing velvet *kamilavka* on their heads, the deacons and altar
boys in brocade vestments. And finally, chasuble glittering,
the Metropolitan himself.

On Christmas night we had only the family at home:
mother, auntie, and the children. And, of course, the
Christmas tree. The tree had a wonderful scent, and the candles gave off their own aroma of wax. The tree was decorated
with gold paper angels and stars, tangled up in silver "rain," or
tinsel. I liked the fat glass pears—they didn't break if they fell.

Of course, we all expected presents. We weren't wealthy,
so we children didn't get big presents, just a few things. Once I
received a watch that didn't run. I was wildly ecstatic—both
because the watch didn't run and because it was mine! My
watch! Another time I got a windup "American" toy, a car.
You wind it up and it goes! It was funny, strange . . . and nice.

*Once Tchaikovsky's publisher presented the composer with a
Christmas surprise: he bought the recently published complete
works of Mozart in seventy-two volumes and asked Alexei,
Tchaikovsky's servant, to put them under the Christmas tree
secretly. Tchaikovsky wrote to his publisher: "Dear friend!
My rapturous gratitude for the best, most precious, marvelous gift that I could ever have hoped to receive! Alexei did
everything you told him, that is, he set up the tree as a surprise and next to it lay my god, my idol, my ideal, represented by all his divine works. I was as happy as a child!"*

Tchaikovsky remained a child all his life, he felt things like a
child. He liked the German idea that man in his highest devel-

184   opment approaches the child. Tchaikovsky loved children as themselves, not as future adults. Children contain maximum possibilities. Those possibilities often do not develop, they are lost.

The Nutcracker at our theater is for children young and old. That is, for children and for adults who are children at heart. Because, if an adult is a good person, in his heart he is still a child. In every person the best, the most important part is that which remains from his childhood.

> Laroche felt that The Nutcracker was a step forward from Sleeping Beauty, because Nutcracker had much less story to it. He wrote, "In the first act of Nutcracker very little happens, but the audience does not sense that: on the stage children dance, argue, and misbehave, and their bustle is artfully and amusingly intertwined with the restrained merriment of the adults."

It is hard for children in the audience to appreciate classical dance. They are used to talking, they need a story. But everything is clear in The Nutcracker, and children like that. Our Nutcracker is more sophisticated than the one in Petersburg; it's closer to the Hoffmann. Our Herr Drosselmeyer is a more important figure. He comes to the party, takes care of the children, but he remains a mysterious person. The children like him, because children adore mysterious characters. Drosselmeyer does tricks for them. I liked it when we were visited by adults who knew how to do tricks. In Petersburg at the ballet school we had children who could do tricks like real magicians.

I did not do Drosselmeyer in Russia, but here I played the part once. Drosselmeyer climbs up on the grandfather clock and does all sorts of tricks. It's that way in Hoffmann—a vi-

sion, a symbol. Drosselmeyer seems to be telling Marie that   185
what she is about to see isn't real, it's a dream. But Marie is
frightened anyway.

Marie has a brother, Fritz, a squabbler. I had a sister, too.
I was a bit older, but we never fought. I was a quiet child, and
she, too, was peace-loving. But when we lived in Finland at the
dacha in winter, the village children would come and pick
fights, calling us nasty names. Then we'd attack them with
snowballs. It felt good—you pack a ball out of crunchy snow
and throw it!

In *The Nutcracker* Fritz and Marie play with the children
who come to their party. I didn't go visiting much when I was
a child. First of all, I didn't have time. Secondly, it was a complicated ritual, visiting in Petersburg. Children did not simply
drop by. Adult males could visit one another, drink and play
cards. But children did it this way: somebody's mother would
come by and invite us for tea, or dinner. Then we went.

Naturally, I had pals, but not special friends. So we did
not give big parties for name days or birthdays. In winter we
were taken to a Christmas party at a special place called the
Bolshoi Hall. Many Petersburg children came. We played
around the tree—we played *rucheyok* [stream, something like
London Bridge] and leapfrog—that was called *slon* [elephant].
We ran and skipped, but we tried not to fall down because we
were all dressed up: velvet, white bows, lace collars. In the
summer, at our dacha in Finland, we played *lapta* [a stick and
ball game].

The son of Eduard Napravnik, musical director of the
Maryinsky Theater, reminisced about how Tchaikovsky
composed The Nutcracker: *"Sometimes at lunch Tchai-*
kovsky would say that he was pleased with his work, other
times he would complain that the work wasn't going well,

Balanchine conducting rehearsal of The Nutcracker, *New York City Ballet*

that he was all 'written out.' Once Tchaikovsky said that at first he had been afraid to write music for ballets because of the strict demands of the ballet master, who would firmly set the number of measures for each dance. But now, Tchaikovsky said, he felt that such ironclad parameters made composing even more interesting for him."

That's exactly what Stravinsky used to say! They're so similar! I know that Tchaikovsky fulfilled Petipa's demands exactly, without any crankiness. He had a professional approach to the work. When I did *The Nutcracker* in New York, I needed an entr'acte. And suddenly I recalled that the violin solo from *Sleeping Beauty* was the theme that is used when the Christmas tree glows in *The Nutcracker*. It's a wonderful melody, with a magnificent upward swelling of sound that leaves you breathless. Tchaikovsky had decided that since no one played the violin solo from *Sleeping Beauty* he might as well use it here, instead of letting such a diamond go to waste!

It's done frequently in ballet. I once invented millions of different things, and now I sometimes think, why should that be lost? Why should I come up with new ideas when I have so many in reserve? Moreover, thirty or forty years ago I was young, and it's easier to choreograph when you're younger. I could demonstrate a lot of things then that I no longer can. I could lift a ballerina, for instance. So now I recall one of my old tricks and I think, ah! I'll put it in a new ballet. Many of my recent works have things that I came up with when I was eighteen. But perhaps back then I did not quite understand what to do with all those ideas, while now I can utilize them wisely.

People do that sort of thing all the time. Take Tchaikovsky, for instance. His "Waltz of the Flowers" from *Nutcracker* is very much like the waltz from the opera *Eugene Onegin*. And Tchaikovsky wasn't the only one to work that

way. Beethoven used the same dance in his *Eroica* Symphony
and in piano variations, and in the ballet about Prometheus.
And Stravinsky did it too. Good composers don't like to see
their work lying idle, going to waste.

Children are always delighted by the scene of the battle
between the Nutcracker and the mice. Tchaikovsky was terri-
fied of mice. I'm not. Of course, I've probably seen more mice
played onstage than mice in real life. Mice are considered to
be mean. Hoffmann described mice as being treacherous and
vengeful. I don't think that they are mean, but they are obviously unpleasant to humans. When I was taken into the ballet school and my hair was shaved off, the other kids called me
"Rat" but not for long. The Russian writer Alexander Grin
wrote a story called "The Ratcatcher." He imagined that Petersburg was overrun by rats after the revolution. A deserted,
abandoned city, with evil rats scurrying through it, trans-
formed by magic into tiny hooligans. It is true that in those
days Petersburg had thousands upon thousands of homeless
urchins. They could mug or kill you. Everyone was afraid of
them. But I wasn't. I was short, too, and young. People were
afraid to go out at night, but I wasn't.

We dancers are braver than is customarily thought. I remember a story that the Petersburg wizard Sollertinsky told
me. He was in love with a ballerina who was in Lopukhov's
"Dance Symphony" with me. Sollertinsky and the ballerina
went walking in Petersburg at night; she was reciting very romantic poetry out loud. Seeing three toughs up ahead, Sollertinsky suggested they turn the corner, but the ballerina
refused. She went on forward, reciting poetry. The muggers
tried to snatch her purse. She used it to hit one on the head
and knocked another down with a swift kick; the third, upon
seeing all this, ran off. Then she took the frightened Sollertinsky by the arm and went on walking and reciting, as if

190   nothing had happened. Sollertinsky confessed sorrowfully that after that walk he fell out of love.

At one time in our *Nutcracker* we had white mice fighting as well as gray ones. I decided to have the white mice running around under the tree, it could be interesting. But, as usual, there wasn't enough time and it didn't work. It confused the audience; people thought that the white mice were the good guys, while in both Hoffmann and Tchaikovsky the mice are evil. So I got rid of the white mice to avoid confusion. In general, this is a traditional scene, after Ivanov's staging. Ballets often show battles and toy soldiers. It's easy to show a toy soldier standing and moving. Toys come off well in ballet. And children like battles.

When I was small, I had a few toy soldiers. They were a present. Other children collected tin soldiers, but I wasn't one of them. But at school we played Robin Hood. And war! We invented a special game, without sabers. We weren't allowed to play with swords and other sharp objects. We could hurt ourselves. And if you were hurt, you couldn't perform. The teachers watched us closely on that, not because they felt sorry for us, but because they didn't want to spoil a performance.

We were forbidden a lot of things at ballet school. We couldn't ski or ice-skate. We couldn't ride bicycles. Or play ball. But we weren't interested in ball games, because the passion for soccer came to Russia much later.

The end of act one of *Nutcracker* is the Waltz of the Snowflakes. Everything is covered with snow. Marie walks in the snow and does not notice that she is missing a slipper. She had thrown one at the Mouse King during the battle. And where would she get another one in the woods?

Tchaikovsky wrote to the director of the Imperial Theaters: "The second act of Nutcracker *can be produced very effectively—but it requires delicate filigree work." Laroche stated:*

"At the end of Nutcracker the authors have created a color-
ful ethnographic exhibit (Spanish, Arabian, Chinese dances,
the Russian trepak, and the French polka and contredanse).
In order to write these dances, Tchaikovsky did not indulge
in musical archaeology, he did not bury himself in a museum
or library; he wrote the music he felt like writing. And, for
instance, his Chinese dancers got by without any signs of
Chinese music. The results were delightful."

Of course there is nothing Chinese in *The Nutcracker*. Tchaikovsky was not interested in the struggle between good and
bad Chinese. His Chinese dance is not Chinese music at all,
it's a wonderful composition by Tchaikovsky. The idea for all
those dances belonged to Petipa. There always was a *divertisse-*
ment in ballet, you needed some dance numbers. And Petipa
suggested Spanish, Arabian, and Russian dances. Tchaikovsky
took a Georgian lullaby for the Arabian dance. It's a Georgian
melody, not Arabian—but who cares? It's a small masterpiece.

The second act of *Nutcracker* is more French than German.
Petipa liked the idea of Konfituerenburg because at the time in
Paris there was a fad for special spectacles in which various
sweets were depicted by dancers. Actually, *Nutcracker's* second
act is an enormous balletic sweetshop. In Petersburg there was
a store like that, it was called Eliseyevsky's: huge glass windows, rooms big enough for a palace, high ceilings, opulent
chandeliers, almost like the ones at the Maryinsky. The floors
at Eliseyevsky's were covered with sawdust, and you could not
hear footsteps—it was like walking on carpets. The store had
sweets and fruits from all over the world, like in *A Thousand*
and One Nights. I used to walk past and look in the windows
often. I couldn't buy anything there, it was too expensive. But I
remember the store as clearly as if I had been staring in the
window just yesterday.

Everything that appears in the second act of *Nutcracker* is a

192   candy or something tasty. Or a toy—like Mère Gigonne with the Polichinelles. The Sugar Plum Fairy is a piece of candy and the dewdrops are made of sugar. The Buffon is a candy cane. It's all sugar!

The Petersburg *Nutcracker* also had Prince Coqueluche. Coqueluche means whooping cough. I think Prince Coqueluche was supposed to represent a lozenge or cough drop. But that wasn't very clear, and so in our production, instead of Prince Coqueluche the Sugar Plum Fairy dances with a cavalier.

All this makes up Konfityerenburg, land of sweets. It was Hoffmann's idea, but Petipa saw that it could be beautiful and interesting in a ballet. The audience doesn't always understand that they are seeing candies and toys onstage and ask, what is that? Maybe it's our own fault that it's not clear, but we tried as hard as we could. They're supposed to make everyone's mouth water!

At the end of the ballet Marie and the Nutcracker, who is now a prince, leave in a sleigh hitched to reindeer. They didn't have reindeer at the Maryinsky. That's my idea, that. The audience loves it. If Marie and the prince rode off on kangaroos instead of reindeer, no one would understand. When you invent something, you must always use what already exists in life instead of indulging in silly fantasies. After all, you can ride reindeer! Everyone responds to it, and that helps create the general mood for this scene. Every detail like that is important in a ballet like *Nutcracker*. You have to do everything gradually, otherwise they'll say, what is this? This never happens! No one does that! We don't understand! You have to accustom audiences to new things a step at a time, so that people don't feel that you consider them idiots.

I think that people also like *Nutcracker* so much because nowadays everyone is interested in how children used to live

and play. In my day there was no interest in that. No one asked children how they lived, what they thought. Children simply tried to become as much like adults as quickly as possible, and that was all.

ELEVEN

Craftsmen

I READ somewhere that Tchaikovsky was sitting working on the Sixth Symphony, the *Pathétique*, and he needed money. Tchaikovsky turned to his publisher for help, who told him: write something simple for the piano, so that amateurs can play it. And you could write some songs, too, I'll pay you well. So Tchaikovsky decided that he would write a piano piece or a song every day. He used to say, "I'm cooking my musical hotcakes." And in two weeks Tchaikovsky wrote eighteen piano pieces and six songs. This after first complaining that the writing wasn't going well; but then he got carried away and worked with incredible speed. And the pieces turned out to be good!

Then Tchaikovsky sent his servant to the publisher with a letter: here, he said, are your pieces and songs; please pay as we agreed, one hundred rubles each. The publisher liked them so much that he paid Tchaikovsky one hundred fifty for each! 195

196 Tchaikovsky later joked that if he had stayed in the country composing for a year he would have been a millionaire.

> *Tchaikovsky wrote to Nadezhda von Meck: "Inspiration is a guest who does not like visiting the lazy. It comes to those who call for it. I write either from an inner impulse, borne by a higher power of inspiration, which doesn't lend itself to analysis, or else I simply* work, *calling for this power. . . ."*

Tchaikovsky was a modest man, but, of course, he knew his own worth—as does every professional. Once when people were talking about some king in his presence, Tchaikovsky said, "In music, I'm king!" But he constantly needed money, he had to pay his rent. And so he took on the most varied commissions. And didn't make a fuss about it at all.

I recently looked at those piano pieces Tchaikovsky "cooked up like hotcakes": a lot of excellent music. I see where he took a bit from Schumann and a bit from Beethoven. Because he had to work fast. And it's remarkable, anyway. We all work on order, we do some things hurriedly. In my life I did thousands of various things. You can do the same thing in different ways, depending on the commission. In Petersburg I was asked to do dances in various theaters, so I worked at the Alexandrinsky Theater with Sergei Radlov on a play by Ernst Toller, and I did *Caesar and Cleopatra* by G. B. Shaw there, too. At the Mikhailovsky Theater I was asked to do the dances for Rimsky-Korsakov's *Coq d'Or.* And once I danced the Polovetsian Dances in *Prince Igor:* there were two of us, a friend and I made up the whole Polovetsian horde. This was in the Iron Hall of the People's House in Petersburg, on the Petrograd side. There was an opera theater for the masses there, a rather poor one. They had almost no funds at all. I remember that the young Andre Kostelanetz conducted there.

And here in the West, I could stage the same piece in dif-

ferent ways. When there are a lot of people, like at the opera, 197
you can do things on a grander scale. But in Monte Carlo I was
forced to be quite ingenious. I remember we staged *Samson et
Dalila* by Saint-Saëns: I did the dances in that for only three
people!

Tchaikovsky said—I write anything at all. If they commission an opera, I'll write an opera; they need a march, here
you go; they need a cantata for some occasion, glad to do it.
We all work like that. And I know that great composers like to
work on commission.

I remember when I worked on Broadway, I had a bit of
money. This must have been in 1940, I guess. After all kinds of
expenses, I still had five hundred dollars left. I thought, what
should I do with the money? Buy some extraordinary cigarette
case or something? And then I decided, ah! I'll ask Hindemith
to write something for me.

In those days I used to give parties for my musician
friends. I always made the *zakuski* [hors d'oeuvres] myself, and
put on the vodka. And then we played music. Back then I had
two grands in the place; my friend Nikolai Kopeikin and I
played on them.

Hindemith was teaching at Yale then, I believe, and living
in New Haven. He had a two-story house with a garden. He
planted flowers and tended fruit trees. I had visited him there.
I told Hindemith, "I have five hundred dollars, could you write
something for me?" Hindemith said, "What would you like?"
I explained that I wanted something for piano and strings.
Hindemith replied, "All right, I have the time now, I'll be glad
to do it." I gave him the money. And a month later he called
and said that he had composed a theme and variations, *The
Four Temperaments.*

I called together musicians I knew. I remember that
Nathan Milstein came, and the cellist Raya Garbuzova, and
Leon Barzin. We ate and drank, and the musicians played the

198   Hindemith, excellently, professionally. Later Hindemith told me, "If you like, you can use that piece for ballet. But I don't want *The Four Temperaments* played in concerts, because I'm writing in another style now." I think he was composing his piano cycle *Ludus Tonalis* then.

I did *The Four Temperaments* as a ballet. But the interesting thing is that now they quite often play this piece at concerts. And even record it. Because Hindemith had written quality music, even though it was commissioned. That's what's called craftsmanship.

Stravinsky also used to say, "I write whatever. For jazz—fine. For movies or TV—fine." He, like Hindemith, found time for me: Stravinsky wrote circus music for me, a polka for elephants. I remember, I had called him and said, "Igor Fyodorovich, I need a polka, could you write it for me?" Stravinsky replied, "Yes, I have the time right now. Who's the polka for?" I explained that my ballerina was an elephant. "Is the elephant ballerina young?" he asked. I said, "Yes, she's not old." Stravinsky laughed and said, "Well, if she's young, that's fine! Then I'll be happy to do it." And he wrote a polka dedicated "to a young elephant ballerina." He wasn't embarrassed to write for the circus.

I recently was told of an extraordinary example of Tchaikovsky's craftsmanship. Anna Sobeshchanskaya, a prima in the Bolshoi Ballet in Tchaikovsky's day, danced in the mediocre Moscow production of *Swan Lake*. In order to liven up her benefit performance Sobeshchanskaya asked Petipa to create a *pas de deux* for her, and she inserted it in the third act of *Swan Lake*. She wasn't worried that Petipa had done the *pas de deux* to music by Minkus!

Learning this, Tchaikovsky protested, "My ballet may be good or bad, but I alone bear the responsibility for its music." Tchaikovsky offered to write a new *pas de deux* for the ballerina, but she did not wish to change Petipa's choreography. So,

taking Minkus' music, Tchaikovsky wrote his own *pas de deux* 199
which fit—measure for measure—the dance Sobeshchanskaya
had already learned. She did not have to relearn anything, not
even rehearse, thanks to Tchaikovsky.

> *Tchaikovsky wrote to Grand Duke Konstantin Romanov:*
> *"Ever since I began writing, I set myself a goal: to be in my*
> *métier what the greatest musical masters—Mozart, Beetho-*
> *ven, Schubert—were in theirs. I mean, not as great a genius*
> *as they are, but like them a composer who works in the man-*
> *ner of a* cobbler *rather than in the manner of a* gentleman
> *of leisure. Mozart, Beethoven, Schubert, Mendelssohn, and*
> *Schumann composed their immortal works exactly the way a*
> *cobbler makes his shoes—day in and day out, and primarily*
> *on order. The results were something colossal." And*
> *Tchaikovsky adds, "A musician, if he wants to achieve the*
> *heights to which he can aspire on the strength of his gift,*
> *must cultivate the* craftsman *in himself."*

I'm afraid that Tchaikovsky will be misunderstood here, taken
literally—that he really wanted to become a cobbler. Neither
Mozart, nor Schumann, nor Tchaikovsky were cobblers! He's
talking about one thing: that you have to work every day.
Some people imagine that you can be sitting around doing
nothing and suddenly a brilliant idea will strike you. It doesn't
happen this way. Tchaikovsky is right in that. Behind every
good idea lies horrible, exhausting work. You knock your
brains out and nothing comes. You see a kind of pile, everything jumbled. And you spend a long, long time raking
through this pile—and still nothing good comes out of it. And
you don't know what to do next. As Pushkin said about his
writing, "Which way shall we sail?" But after you've worked
hard enough, the work gradually starts taking shape. And then
you look to see if it's all done in the right way. Because every

200   profession and skill has its rules, and they must be obeyed. Say you want to learn French. First you must know French grammar and the like. Otherwise, you'll make all kinds of silly mistakes, and they'll laugh at you! So in your own work, first you obey certain rules, and then you start coming up with your own ideas. Then you can think, Is what I'm doing interesting? Maybe I can come up with some unusual jump or a different angle? You think, will this be effective? You could say that in general there are certain rules in art, but no laws. You must know the rules and you may break the laws.

> *Tchaikovsky wrote to the Grand Duke: "Not everything long is drawn-out; verbosity is not necessarily claptrap, and brevity is not at all a condition for absolute beauty of form. Literal repetitions, hardly acceptable in literature, are absolutely necessary in music."*

It's the same in ballet. It's not necessary to keep inventing new movements all the time. You can repeat them, there's no sin in that. The audience ordinarily does not notice repetition, but that's not the point. Repetition is good for the construction of a piece. Tchaikovsky understood that. He built his compositions skillfully, but in his own way. Bach did it by one set of rules, and Tchaikovsky by others. Tchaikovsky would have felt caged in Bach's forms.

Tchaikovsky, like any artist, wanted the public to love his music. Only a madman would think, Well, I'm going to invent something so crazy that the public will be certain to hate it! We all want our work to be appreciated.

Tchaikovsky once said about a certain young composer that he had real talent because he was not afraid of being trite in his music. Clearly, Tchaikovsky meant himself. It's not a question of triteness, of course, but of not being afraid to write music that the public will like. Mozart's father wrote to him,

Rehearsing with Suzanne Farrell and Jacques d'Amboise

"You must become popular." And Mozart tried, he sought interesting librettos for his operas. And is there anyone who would say that Mozart wrote trite music? Stravinsky did not demean his talent when he wrote a polka for a young elephant. These composers were not snobs, that's why they achieved so much.

TWELVE

Stravinsky

NOT many people know that Igor Fyodorovich Stravinsky loved Tchaikovsky's music. Stravinsky told me many times of his reverence for Tchaikovsky. Tchaikovsky and Stravinsky are two composers who wrote great music especially for us dancers. Of course, Ravel also should not be forgotten. I knew Ravel, we met when I was doing his *L'Enfant et les sortilèges* in 1925 for the Opera de Monte Carlo. It was its premiere. But back then, to tell the truth, I did not understand Ravel's music quite so well. And I didn't understand French at all. Ravel did not impress me very much then—just a short gentleman, elegantly dressed. It's only now that I realize what a great composer he was. He wrote an opulent ballet—*Daphnis et Chloë*. And, of course, compositions like *La Valse* and *Valses nobles et sentimentales*.

There is a stupid idea about Stravinsky: that he is a cerebral composer whose music is too complex and calculated. 203

204 Actually Stravinsky's music is jolly, springy, very danceable. Stravinsky was never an old man. I always think of him as a young fellow. Stravinsky was a joyous person. When we worked together, we always had a good time.

> *Tchaikovsky knew Igor Stravinsky's father, Fyodor Stravinsky (1843–1902), a bass at the Maryinsky Theater, very well and appreciated his talent. Fyodor Stravinsky was in the Kiev premiere of Tchaikovsky's opera* The Oprichnik; *recalling the Kiev performance, Tchaikovsky wrote about Stravinsky, ". . . his marvelous voice and lively acting brought the not-particularly rich or thankful part of Vyazminsky into the foreground." Stravinsky also sang in the Petersburg premieres of other Tchaikovsky operas:* The Maid of Orleans, Mazeppa, *and* The Sorceress. *Stravinsky's performance as the monk Mamyrov in* The Sorceress *was particularly successful.* Peterburgskii listok *wrote: "M. Stravinsky performed his small monologue, 'Me, me he forced to dance' with such stunning drama that he brought forth a storm of applause from the whole theater and shouts of encore." Tchaikovsky, who had conducted the premiere, gave the singer his picture with the inscription "To Fyodor Ignatievich Stravinsky from an admirer of his talent who is deeply grateful for his marvelous performance of the part of Mamyrov. 3 November 1887." Igor Stravinsky remembered that "this photograph was the most treasured object in my father's studio."*

If Igor Stravinsky is correct when he says that the Counts Litke were cousins of his mother, then he himself should have been a distant relative of Tchaikovsky's: Counts Alexander and Konstantin Litke were Tchaikovsky's cousin's nephews. According to the Soviet editors of Tchaikovsky's letters (Moscow, 1978, volume XVIA), Alexander/Sanya/Litke "was part of the group of young people jokingly called Tchaikovsky's 'fourth suite,'" which is a pun on the Russian words suita *(suite) and* svita *(entourage).*

Stravinsky loved Tchaikovsky's ballets most of all. He felt that
Tchaikovsky invented incredible melodies—and not just the
melodies per se, but also their fabulous harmonization and
orchestration. Stravinsky used to say, "You can find such marvelous things in Tchaikovsky and Gounod!" Tchaikovsky's
Mozartiana, certainly, was an influence on Stravinsky's pastiches. And, of course, one of the most famous of his pastiches
is *Le Baiser de la fée,* a ballet that was Stravinsky's "Tchaikovskyana." Stravinsky found the story in Hans Christian Andersen's fairy tales, but that's not important; what is important is
that the ballet is a homage to Tchaikovsky. In it Stravinsky
used themes from a dozen or so compositions by Tchaikovsky, primarily the piano pieces, but also the songs and
even a few things from the operas. Some of the themes are
quite familiar—"Lullaby in a Storm," for instance. Or the
piano piece, *Feuillet d'album.* But there are "quotes" which only
people like me hear, because we know Tchaikovsky's music
well—from his *Children's Album,* from *Queen of Spades,* or from
another opera, *Cherevichki.* I even hear echoes from Tchaikovsky's First Symphony in that Stravinsky ballet.

I hear something of Tchaikovsky in Stravinsky's ballet
Apollo, too. In the Prologue the strings sound quite "Tchai-
kovskyian," and the same is true of a few other places. I think
that while he was composing *Apollo,* Stravinsky thought about
Tchaikovsky's *Sleeping Beauty.* I also hear Tchaikovsky in other
works by Stravinsky, sometimes at the most unexpected moments. Well, seeking similarities in the music of two great
composers is a pointless exercise. The important thing is that
Stravinsky understood ballet as well as Tchaikovsky did. He
told me: "Ballet is a performance. People watch! A boy sits in
the first row, he wants to look at the girl onstage. It should be
interesting for him." Stravinsky understood that you can't
write boring music for ballet. Everything has to move

206   smoothly and swiftly—tempo, tempo! Like an express train, without stopping at unimportant stations.

> *The Russian composer Arthur Lourié, who in the midtwen-*
> *ties was Stravinsky's influential friend and, in the words of*
> *Robert Craft, his "musical coadjutant," wrote in 1927:*
> *"The certain similarity between Stravinsky and Tchaikovsky*
> *is based on the fact that there exists an almost familylike*
> *'musical blood resemblance,' for all the differences in tem-*
> *perament and taste. . . . Stravinsky had to connect himself*
> *with Tchaikovsky, it was a natural reaction against out-*
> *dated modernism. The always present connection between*
> *Stravinsky and Tchaikovsky was consciously revealed by*
> *Stravinsky in* Mavra *and later in the* Octet for Wind In-
> *struments."*

I did not come to understand all of Stravinsky's music immediately. Once upon a time I had liked Rachmaninoff's music. I
always tried to catch all of Rachmaninoff's concerts in Petersburg. He was a keyboard genius! When I came to the West
from Russia, Danilova and I tried to get to one of his concerts
at the very first opportunity. It was in London. We sat and listened to the Chopin and Schumann. He played brilliantly!
Then his own works. We liked them!

After the concert we went to see Rachmaninoff in the
green room. Tons of people, all waiting in line. Rachmaninoff
stood in the corner, tall, glum. His fans came over one after the
other, bugging out their eyes, shouting compliments. The procession moved slowly, slowly. Finally, our turn came. We
came up to Rachmaninoff, we bowed, how do you do, it was
so wonderful! I said, "This is Danilova from the Maryinsky,
and I'm Balanchivadze. We're dancers from the Maryinsky
Theater. We're ecstatic! We always come to your concerts!
You're a great pianist!" Rachmaninoff was silent. I went on

Diaghilev, 1908 portrait by Valentin Serov

humbly, "If you would only allow, I would like to ask you re-spectfully—" Rachmaninoff interrupted me rudely: "What?" I tried to continue, "Your marvelous *Elegy* ... Perhaps you would permit me to do something with your music ... for dancing...." Rachmaninoff began shouting, "Have you lost your mind?! You're crazy! Dance to my music? How dare you? Get out! Get out!" We apologized, bowed, and ran away.

We were nobodies, just dancers, garbage. And he was a great pianist, a genius. I liked his music then. But my thanks to

Sergei Rachmaninoff

Diaghilev, he set me straight. I once said something about Rachmaninoff . . . and Diaghilev told me, "My dear fellow, *go-lubchik*, don't be silly, it's terrible music! There are many wonderful composers in the world, but Rachmaninoff isn't one of them. You have to develop some taste. Forget about Rachmaninoff!" I said, "All right." And I did.

Of course Diaghilev was right. Rachmaninoff's music is mush, especially the orchestral works. But even his piano music is horrible. His Variations on a Theme by Corelli—it's a

Sergei Prokofiev

salad, a *macedoine*, nonsense. No, I don't like Rachmaninoff anymore.

Scriabin—that's something else, he has interesting works for the piano. The piano sonatas are very, very good. But take his piano concerto: it starts out in an attractive way, quite beautifully, and then wham, there's nothing left, it's all over. And from then on it's painfully uninteresting. Scriabin's symphonies are terribly orchestrated. And I also don't like all the pretension in his works, the attempts to philosophize. That

210   makes Scriabin's music literally fall apart. Philosophy is a different thing, why take it up in music?

Diaghilev wasn't a great admirer of Scriabin's music, but,
as I remember, he respected him personally. He appreciated
Prokofiev's talent but did not care much for his opinions. Prokofiev in fact was a terrible *retrograde*. I did his ballet *Prodigal
Son* for Diaghilev. It's a biblical story, but the music was, of
course, quite modern. And I did what I thought would be best
for the music. Diaghilev really liked my ideas, he kept saying,
"marvelous, marvelous." But Prokofiev, when he came to a rehearsal, began shouting that it was all horrible, he disagreed
completely with it all. Well, Prokofiev did not understand a
thing about dance. He didn't care about choreography at all.
Actually, he didn't care how his ballet was staged, it was all
the same to him. But when Prokofiev was composing his *Prodigal Son*, he had this idea that it would all be realistic-looking
onstage: bearded men sitting and drinking real wine out of
real goblets, the dancers dressed with "historical accuracy." In
a word, Prokofiev imagined the *Prodigal Son* somewhat like *Ri-
goletto*. And, of course, he was horrified by my staging. Prokofiev hated what I had done to his music. And Diaghilev,
naturally, yelled at Prokofiev that he didn't understand a thing
about ballet, that he was an absolute idiot. And Prokofiev had
to shut up, because it was Diaghilev's parade.

This was followed by another incident with Prokofiev.
France had La Société des auteurs et compositeurs dramatiques. They paid royalties. If a ballet was performed, the
composer got two thirds of the royalties and the librettist a
third. If the librettist was someone very important, then, perhaps, he went half and half with the composer. But for that the
librettist had to be some genius, a big man. The libretto for
Prodigal Son had been written by Boris Kochno, Diaghilev's
secretary. He made good money by scribbling up little stories
for various ballets and getting his part of the royalties for

them. But nobody cared about us dancers. We did not belong
to La Société des auteurs. We were just ballet people, fools.
We did not belong among wise men. And at that time I was so
badly paid by Diaghilev, so little—just pennies. You couldn't
live on the money. We were always starving. I had several
pairs of trousers, and I remember I went to the Marché aux
puces, the Paris flea market, sold a pair, and bought sausages.
And we all lived on those sausages.

In desperation I went to Kochno: "Could you perhaps
give me some money? I worked on *Prodigal Son* a long time.
And I need money very badly." Kochno explained that he got
only one third and Prokofiev two thirds, and that I should go
ask Prokofiev. I went off to see Prokofiev. He started shouting
at me: "What did you ever do? It's all nonsense, what you did!
The *Prodigal Son* is mine! Why should you be paid? Who are
you? Get out of here! I won't give you anything!"

A terrible man, that Prokofiev. He could have said, "You
know, my dear man, *golubchik*, I need money myself now, I
can't share with you." Or something like that. No—he had to
shout at me as if I were a boy. I apologized, bowed, and left
quietly.

Rachmaninoff disliked Stravinsky very much. He felt that
Stravinsky was stealing his fame. As if you could take fame
away from Rachmaninoff! And it seemed to me that the success of Stravinsky's music bothered Prokofiev, too.

Diaghilev not only helped me to understand the subtleties
of Stravinsky's music, he explained painting to me, too. He
opened my eyes to Botticelli. We were in Florence together.
Diaghilev led me to the Uffizi Gallery, sat me in front of Botticelli's *La Primavera*, and said, "Look at it." Then he went off
with Lifar and Kochno to have lunch. It wasn't very nice on his
part. When Diaghilev returned to the Uffizi, full, I was sitting
in front of the Botticelli, hungry and angry. Diaghilev asked
me, "Well, do you understand anything?" Of course I had

212   seen that *La Primavera* was a wonderful painting, but I was angry with Diaghilev. Lifar and Kochno were his favorites, he dressed them well and fed them well. And, of course, they played at being great connoisseurs of art. To spite Diaghilev, I said that I didn't understand a thing: well, a painting like any other, so what? Nothing special. Diaghilev lost his temper then. But actually I had liked Botticelli very much. And his *Primavera* has stayed with me for my whole life.

Natasha Makarova recently sent me a Christmas card, and on it is Botticelli's *Primavera*. Reminding people of spring in winter is clever. I know that Natasha wants that card to suggest a ballet idea to me. She somehow realized that I liked Botticelli. That's female intuition.

Still, even though I have worked with many now-famous artists, I don't get my ideas from looking at paintings. I worked with Georges Rouault, Utrillo, Matisse, and André Derain, but they had no influence on me. I simply did my job. But I was friends with some artists. I had a very good relationship with Pavlik Tchelitchev; he was incredibly talented, a brilliant painter. Temperamental, of course, but who of us isn't? I was friends with the German artist Max Ernst. He lived here in New York. I met him in Monte Carlo, at Diaghilev's. Ernst did two surrealistic curtains for one of Diaghilev's ballets. I enjoyed looking at Ernst's collages.

When I do ballets, I do not depend heavily on the artist's work. Petipa didn't either. Diaghilev sometimes felt that decor was the most important element in a production. Maybe that's because Diaghilev had worked with Mikhail Fokine, and Fokine liked to stylize things. Fokine was always excited by some paintings and drawings, by all kinds of decorative things—interiors, they were very important for him, costumes. For his time Fokine was a very important ballet master, he put on lots of interesting ballets. Petipa had everything figured out along straight lines: the soloists in front, the corps de ballet in back.

But Fokine invented curved lines in ballet. He also invented 213
the ensemble in ballet. Fokine took a small ensemble and
made up interesting, strange things for it. I knew Fokine before the revolution, in the Maryinsky Theater. He played guitar and mandolin well. Fokine was a famous man, and I was a
small kid. It was interesting dancing in his ballets. But he was
mean, always cursing. His wife was also a dancer—a beautiful
Jewish woman, a real Jewish princess, and so curvaceous. But
she wasn't good enough to be a prima ballerina, even though
Fokine tried to make her one.

Fokine first collaborated with Diaghilev and Stravinsky
and then had a falling out with them. Then he began working
with Rachmaninoff, who did not like Stravinsky. In his last
years, Fokine attacked Diaghilev, maintaining that the latter
knew nothing about ballet. According to him, even Telyakovsky, director of the Imperial Theaters before the revolution, knew more about ballet than Diaghilev. Telyakovsky I
saw at the Maryinsky. He was an important gentleman, always
well dressed. They said he was a former officer of the Guards.
Perhaps, Telyakovsky did know something about ballet, I
can't judge. But Diaghilev was a real connoisseur, that I can
say with certainty. Especially since in those days there wasn't
very much to understand in ballet, it was a quite simple thing.

Of course, Diaghilev was not a ballet professional, but he
spent a lot of time with ballet people, with Anna Pavlova and
Nijinsky, when they were in class. Diaghilev always asked
them, why do you do this this way and this that way? And he
thought, ah! that's the way it should be. Also, Diaghilev really
understood music. He wasn't simply an impressive-looking
man, he was eager to listen to professional musicians when
they spoke. And he caught on with fantastic speed. Because all
that—music and dance—was very dear to him.

Nijinsky, of course, was magnificent. He literally flew
through the air, powerfully, not like angels do, but our way,

214 like ballet people do. They call it "Nijinsky's secret"; but a lot of Nijinsky's technique is accessible to other dancers. I can put it this way: one dancer can do one thing well, and another something else; there may be a dancer who can leap like Nijinsky, and another may be able to do another thing from Nijinsky's bag of tricks. But only Nijinsky could do them all! He could do everything! And that was his secret.

People argue over whether Nijinsky was a good choreographer. What I saw was promising. I would say that he could have become a real ballet master if he had been given the chance. Nijinsky knew how to invent interesting things. They should have asked for more new ballets from him, he should have been commissioned more frequently. Nijinsky did his ballets to complicated music, it was too hard for him. Still, I think that Nijinsky was more talented than his sister Bronislava, even though she did a few interesting things herself. Of course, I probably would have done Stravinsky's *Les Noces* differently from what she did.

No one has a monopoly on Stravinsky's music. It can be done in different ways. Maybe some achieve more interesting results than others. Here the public rules. The same with Tchaikovsky: They did *Swan Lake* horribly in Moscow, then Petipa produced *Swan Lake* in St. Petersburg and the public loved it. Isadora Duncan danced to the music of the Sixth Symphony, the *Pathétique*. She danced exactly the same way to the *Marseillaise* and the *Internationale*. She didn't care to which music she jumped, as long as her scarves exposed her body. Fokine did Tchaikovsky's *Serenade* for strings, he called it *Eros*. I didn't like it very much, so I did *Serenade* my own way. Maybe tomorrow someone will decide that my *Serenade* isn't very interesting after all and will do it his way. If the public likes it, then let his *Serenade* run.

When I was still in Petersburg, I wanted to stage Stravinsky's *Pulcinella*. Volodya Dmitriev had some interesting ideas on it. We argued, and sometimes Lopukhov himself joined in. The only time we were afraid of Lopukhov was during rehearsals, when he was capable of shouting something quite offensive. When we were discussing the future of ballet, or new music, we weren't in the least afraid of Lopukhov, even though he was our boss. In the corridor of the Maryinsky Theater I could disagree with him as much as I liked. Lopukhov found our company stimulating. But when I asked him for permission to do *Pulcinella*, it turned out that it was impossible. They had to pay in *valuta* [hard currency] for the score, and they had none. After I left Petersburg for Europe, I learned that *Pulcinella* had indeed been done at the Maryinsky, by Lopukhov and Dmitriev. It's like Gogol wrote: "There wasn't room in the church for an apple to fall. The mayor came in— and room was found." So they found the hard currency for *Pulcinella* but without me.

> *Alexandre Benois recalled how the impression made by* Sleeping Beauty *led the Petersburg cognoscenti to take an interest in ballet: "Tchaikovsky seemed to be opening doors for me through which I could go deeper and deeper into the past. This past became even closer and more understandable than the present. The magic of music convinced me that I was 'coming home.' . . . My delight with* Sleeping Beauty *returned me to the ballet, and I passed my passion to all my friends. I am sure that if I had not fallen madly in love with* Sleeping Beauty *and not spread my enthusiasm to my friends, there would have been no Ballets Russes nor the* balletomania *created by its success."*

It's hard for me now to imagine that Diaghilev and Stravinsky needed to be convinced of the merits of *Sleeping Beauty*. That's a different world. But I do remember, of course, that in Russia many considered Tchaikovsky a not-very-Russian composer.

Stravinsky, conducting in Leningrad during his triumphant 1962 return to Russia

It was fashionable to say that the Russian composers were Mussorgsky and Rimsky-Korsakov. Well, really Rimsky-Korsakov was a very learned gentleman. I have his textbook on orchestration, which shows the range for every instrument: it's convenient for the clarinet to play from here to here, and for the cello from here to here. If you orchestrate according to Rimsky-Korsakov, it will sound good, marvelous. (Rimsky-Korsakov orchestrated two Mussorgsky operas that way; they say he "spruced it up." Stravinsky, with Ravel, orchestrated Mussorgsky's *Khovanshchina* on a commission from Diaghilev.) Time passes and now, I think, Tchaikovsky is considered no less a Russian composer than Mussorgsky. And Stravinsky

has been acknowledged in Russia now. While here, we always   217
knew Stravinsky was a real Russian composer.

Stravinsky, like Tchaikovsky, was a hard worker. He always followed a strict schedule. That's very important! That's why Stravinsky succeeded so well. Now, when I think about Stravinsky, I see that he did everything right, while I often went astray. I wanted one thing but then would come up with something entirely different—neither fish nor fowl. Sometimes I should have stopped and thought, just sat quietly, but I didn't have the time. And sometimes it seemed we were doing the right thing, but it didn't come out right. Stravinsky planned, and I improvised. That may be my great fault.

I did many projects with Stravinsky. He played his *Apollon Musagète*, which in Greek means Apollo, leader of the Muses, at rehearsals. Now the ballet is simply called *Apollo*. I did *Le Baiser de la fée*, Stravinsky's "Tchaikovskyana," and also his *Jeu de cartes*. We did those two ballets at the Met. We worked on *Orpheus* and *Agon* together from the start. That's the way it should be, the way Petipa worked with Tchaikovsky.

In our theater, we did many ballets to Stravinsky's music. We tried to perform it as often as possible, so the public would have an opportunity to listen to Stravinsky's music. Before, Stravinsky was not played frequently, if you don't count three of his early major works—*Firebird, Petrouchka,* and *Sacre du printemps*. People were used to those works and liked them but not the later compositions. They made excuses: "Yes, well, he may be a great composer, but we don't understand him." They said, "We don't need it; now *Sacre du printemps*, that's another story." As for his other work: "Maybe it's good, but it's not for us." But now they're used to Stravinsky and they like his music. They say, "How could we have not understood it before?" Now it's easy to say "Stravinsky? A genius!" Well, I knew that sixty years ago, when it wasn't so easy to figure out.

Tchaikovsky, 1893

THIRTEEN

"Russian Roulette"

CHAIKOVSKY was thinking about a name for his Sixth Symphony, which he had just finished. His brother first suggested *"Tragique"*; Tchaikovsky didn't like it. But as soon as his brother came up with *"Pathétique,"* Tchaikovsky agreed. He did not want to explain to outsiders why he agreed to name his symphony that, he merely hinted—wait, you'll find out later.

The first movement of the Sixth is short and shattering: like a blizzard. The woodwinds appear like lightning, the orchestration is incredible. And then comes the burial hymn "Repose the Soul." No one, absolutely no one knows that! Maybe someone tells a conductor, look, here is a special part. But you have to know and feel it from your heart. In Soviet Russia they don't speak about it anymore. Only people from the past, like me, understand what that really means: that "Repose the Soul" is sung only when someone has died. A bier stands in the church, the coffin lid is open, and when the service is coming to an end, everyone kneels and weeps: this 219

220 man is *dead!* "Repose the soul of your deceased servant with the saints." It's more than an *Ave Maria* or *Ave Verum*. This begs the saints up in heaven to grant peace to the soul of the deceased. Tchaikovsky wrote that about himself! There's a whirlwind flying through it, a whirlwind! And then down, down, the horns with oboes and bassoons. And suddenly: "Repose the soul." Everybody's crying.

And in the finale of the *Pathétique* there is a soft, other-worldly chorale—three trombones and a tuba. The melody goes down, down, dies out: strings, then woodwinds. Everything stops, as if a man is going into the grave. Going . . . going . . . gone. The end. Tchaikovsky had written his own requiem!

> *Tchaikovsky conducted the first performance of his Sixth Symphony in St. Petersburg. After the concert Tchaikovsky took home his cousin Anna Merkling. On the way he asked if she had understood what he wanted to say in his music. The cousin replied that it seemed to her that in the symphony Tchaikovsky had described his life. "You're right," Tchaikovsky said, and began explaining the symphony's program. According to Merkling, Tchaikovsky said that the first movement dealt with his childhood and his early attempts to compose; in the second, there were scenes of his youth; in the third—life's struggle and the achievement of fame. "Well, the last movement," Tchaikovsky added, "that's the De Profundis, how we all end up."*

Tchaikovsky composed *Pathétique* very quickly, in a little over twenty days. Such an enormous work! After that he conducted the symphony in Petersburg, and no one liked it. But Tchaikovsky didn't care. And a few days later came the announcement: Tchaikovsky is gravely ill. And a few days after that, that he was dead of cholera! But was that the truth? Back in Petersburg I had heard a story that Tchaikovsky hadn't died of

cholera at all but had committed suicide. Because in those
days a man could not reveal that he loved another man. Those
things were forbidden. In England, a few years later, Oscar
Wilde was jailed for that. And they were even stricter about it
in Russia.

They also said that Tchaikovsky was threatened with a
major scandal: Some dignitary was about to complain to the
tsar that Tchaikovsky was involved with the dignitary's son.
Tchaikovsky was an incredibly sensitive and vulnerable man.
He imagined the suffering this would entail. And he obviously
preferred poison.

Tchaikovsky was in a restaurant with his brother and
some friends. He pointedly asked the waiter for a glass of tap
water. There was a cholera epidemic in St. Petersburg at the
time. His brother begged Tchaikovsky not to drink the un-
boiled water. But Tchaikovsky drank it in one gulp, so that his
brother couldn't stop him.

> Laroche recalled that Tchaikovsky "had an inordinate fear
> of death; he was afraid of everything that reminded him of
> death. You could not use words like 'coffin,' 'grave,' or 'fu-
> neral' in front of Tchaikovsky." Laroche continues: "Tchai-
> kovsky depended heavily on hygiene, at which he was a true
> virtuoso. He had observed himself carefully and had deter-
> mined what was healthful for him and what wasn't; and on
> the basis of his self-observations Tchaikovsky went on a
> strict regimen."

Could a man as health conscious and nervous as Tchaikovsky
have drunk tap water during a cholera epidemic? And besides,
he had always suffered from stomach problems. He was always writing in his letters, "I had terrible diarrhea today."
Very much like Glinka, who frequently complained of indigestion in his memoirs. That's quite understandable. Now we

222   keep meat in refrigerators, but they didn't have them, of course. I remember that in Petersburg my mother kept meat outside the window in winter, she had a special device for that. It was the only way to prevent it from spoiling.

Tchaikovsky always kept Vichy tablets in his pocket, and as soon as he felt something was wrong with his stomach, he took soda. He was very concerned about his indigestion. He would not have drunk tap water under any circumstance, and here was an epidemic in Petersburg, people dying all around of cholera.

Did Tchaikovsky take poison? Then his demonstrative behavior in the restaurant was camouflage; look, I just drank choleric water! And then he went home and took poison.

But another explanation is possible. What if Tchaikovsky was playing with fate? If he drank the tap water as if playing a kind of Russian roulette: will I get cholera or won't I?

Tchaikovsky mused a lot about fate and predestination. That's not surprising; he was a true Russian. Russians believe in fate, *fatum*. There's a good reason why that infamous game with the pistol in which fate decides whether it's loaded or not, whether it will shoot or go click, is called Russian roulette. In Tchaikovsky's day the game was very popular among Russian officers.

But most important, Russian literature always made heroes of desperate gamblers. Pushkin described one in *The Queen of Spades*. Pushkin has a novella called *The Shot*, which is also about fate and luck. And then, of course, came Mikhail Lermontov, whom Tchaikovsky adored. No one knows Lermontov here, but in Russia he's revered equally with Pushkin. We studied all his works in school; I memorized Lermontov's *Demon*. Tchaikovsky wrote a song to Lermontov's poem "Love of a Dead Man."

Lermontov's novel *A Hero of Our Time* is very popular and famous in Russia. One of its parts is called "The Fatalist." It's a

Tchaikovsky's funeral in St. Petersburg—October 27, 1893

powerful description of the game of Russian roulette. Tchaikovsky loved *A Hero of Our Time* and reread it often. Well, it's
a very Russian thing—to stake your life on a card, to take a
deadly risk! Maybe Tchaikovsky thought, Ah! I'll see what
happens to me! if everything's all right, it's the will of God.

Of course, Tchaikovsky was a very devout man. And suicide is a major sin. But I read a letter of Tchaikovsky's in

Statue over
Tchaikovsky's tomb
at the St. Alexander
Nevsky Monastery
in St. Petersburg

which he says that he does not believe in a punishing God.
Tchaikovsky wrote that he would like to set to music Christ's
words that "My yoke is sweet and My burden is light." That
is, Tchaikovsky believed and hoped that God would forgive
him.

Still, he would have had to hesitate when contemplating
suicide. In those terrible days for Tchaikovsky when he was
married, he also thought about suicide, but he rejected it. Instead Tchaikovsky tried to catch cold, to chill himself to death.
And that's not the same thing as committing suicide.

There were these people in Russia, hermits. They were
like saints, they lived alone, in small monasteries. They would
lie down in a coffin and stop eating and drinking—and they
would die. This wasn't considered suicide. These hermits believed that they were obeying the will of God. And they died
in peace.

I think that Tchaikovsky had thought about ending his
life somehow for a long time. And I believe that he wrote the
Pathétique Symphony as a kind of suicide note. He wrote it,
then conducted the symphony himself; it was like coming
back to life to see what people would say. He was preparing
himself for his death.

You can't kill yourself by your own hand, that's a sin.
And you can't end your life in despair, suddenly: "Ah, I'm
bored, enough!" Tchaikovsky did not do that. He had walked
a long path. He was afraid of old age, of infirmity. He worried
that he was all written out. He thought that he was beginning
to repeat himself in his music. That wasn't so, of course, but
it's not for us to judge Tchaikovsky. He knew what he was
doing, and he acted as he saw fit.

Tchaikovsky was a noble person. He did not want to in-
volve people dear to him in a scandal. He couldn't stand gossip around his name. Tchaikovsky gave in to society's

226   pressure, accepted its cruel laws—and left this life. They
forced him to die.

How it happened exactly we don't know, and we may
never find out. But is that so important? In order to understand
Tchaikovsky's music, it's enough just to know that a major
tragedy occurred.

> *When he was twenty-one, Tchaikovsky wrote to his sister:
> "How will I end up? What does the future hold? It's terrify-
> ing even to consider. I know that sooner or later (and proba-
> bly sooner) I will not be able to struggle with the difficult side
> of this life and will smash myself into pieces. . . ."*

People forget that Tchaikovsky died at a comparatively young
age. After all, he was only fifty-three.

Adagio Lamentoso, *from Tchaikovsky's Sixth* (Pathétique) *Symphony*

CHRONOLOGIES

Peter Ilyich Tchaikovsky
1840–1893

The purpose of these brief chronologies of Tchaikovsky and Balanchine is to help the reader place in time their relevant works as well as some related names and important events of Russian cultural and political history. The birthdates of Tchaikovsky and Balanchine, and the date of Tchaikovsky's death, are given according to the Julian (Old Style) Calendar used officially in Russia until 1923. The Gregorian (New Style) dates of general Western usage are given in parentheses.

1840

On April 25 (May 7) Peter Ilyich Tchaikovsky is born in the city of Votkinsk.

Mikhail Glinka's vocal cycle *Farewell to Petersburg*. Nikolai Gogol writes volume one of *Dead*

228   *Souls* in Rome. Mikhail Lermontov's novel *A
                       Hero of Our Time.*

1850

Arrives with mother in St. Petersburg. Enter School of Jurisprudence.

First performance of Glinka's *Kamarinskaya*
and *Jota aragonesa* in Petersburg. Six-year-old
Rimsky-Korsakov begins music studies. Ivan
Turgenev's play *A Month in the Country.*

1854

First composition—*Anastasie Valse,* for piano. Mother dies of cholera.

Leo Tolstoy's novella *Youth.* British, French,
and Turkish troops land in the Crimea and
besiege Sevastopol.

1861

First trip abroad (Berlin, London, and Paris).

Emperor Alexander II abolishes serfdom in
Russia. A demonstration of thousands in
Warsaw is dispersed by Russian troops.

1862

Enters newly opened St. Petersburg Conservatory. Meets Hermann
Laroche.

Turgenev publishes *Fathers and Sons.*

1865

Graduates from St. Petersburg Conservatory with the silver medal.

Rimsky-Korsakov's First Symphony performed in St. Petersburg (conducted by Mili
Balakirev). Tolstoy's novel *War and Peace*
begins magazine publication. Alexander Glazunov is born. Russian troops take Tashkent.

1866

Symphony no. 1 (*Winter Daydreams*). Moves to Moscow at invitation
of Nikolai Rubinstein. Teaches at the newly opened Moscow Conservatory.

Dostoyevsky's novel *Crime and Punishment*.
Birth of Leon Bakst and Wassily Kandinsky.

1868

Opera *Voyevoda*. Travels abroad (Berlin, Paris). Meets Rimsky-Korsakov one evening at Balakirev's.

Dostoyevsky's novel *The Idiot*.

1869

Opera *Undine*. Overture fantasy *Romeo and Juliet*. Six songs, opus 6.

Balakirev's piano fantasy *Islamey*. Alexander
Borodin begins opera *Prince Igor*. Marius Petipa
appointed chief ballet master of the Imperial
Maryinsky Theater.

1870

Piano pieces, opuses 7, 8, and 9. Travels abroad (Paris, Switzerland,
Vienna).

Alexandre Benois born in St. Petersburg. Vladimir Ulyanov (Lenin) born in Simbirsk.

230   1871
String Quartet no. 1. Hires Anatoly Sofronov as servant. Travels abroad (Berlin, Paris, Nice.)

> Opera committee of the Maryinsky Theater rejects Mussorgsky's opera *Boris Godunov.*

1872
Symphony no. 2. Opera *The Oprichnik.* Songs, opus 16.

> Mussorgsky begins work on opera *Khovansh-china.* Dostoyevsky's novel *The Possessed.* Laroche becomes professor at St. Petersburg Conservatory. Serge Diaghilev is born.

1873
Symphonic fantasy *The Tempest* (after Shakespeare). Six piano pieces, opus 19. Travels abroad (Dresden, Cologne, Zurich, Berne, Turin, Milan, Paris).

> Premiere of Rimsky-Korsakov's opera *The Maid of Pskov* at Maryinsky Theater. Sergei Rachmaninoff is born.

1874
String Quartet no. 2. Opera *Vakula the Smith* (revised 1885 as *Chere-vichki*).

> Premiere of Mussorgsky's opera *Boris Godunov* at Maryinsky Theater. Mussorgsky's vocal cycle *Without the Sun* and the piano suite *Pic-tures at an Exhibition.* Vsevolod Meyerhold and Nicholas Roerich are born.

1875
Piano Concerto no. 1. Symphony no. 3. Begins work on ballet *Swan*

Lake and *Sérénade mélancholique* for violin and orchestra. Travels   231
abroad (Berlin, Geneva, Paris).

> Composer Sergei Taneyev graduates from
> Tchaikovsky's class at Moscow Conservatory.
> Mussorgsky begins vocal cycle *Songs and
> Dances of Death.*

1876
Finishes *Swan Lake.* Fantasy *Francesca da Rimini* (from Dante's *Divine
Comedy*). Rococo Variations for cello and orchestra. Twelve pieces
for piano, *The Seasons.* String Quartet no. 3. Begins correspondence
with Nadezhda von Meck. Meets Leo Tolstoy. Travels abroad
(Vienna, Vichy, Paris, Bayreuth). Meets Richard Wagner and Franz
Liszt.

> Borodin finished Symphony no. 2. Tolstoy's
> novel *Anna Karenina* begins magazine publica-
> tion.

1877
Symphony no. 4. Valse Scherzo for violin and orchestra. Premiere of
Swan Lake at the Bolshoi Theater. Marriage to Antonina Milyukova,
separation same year. Monthly subsidy from Nadezhda von Meck
begins. Travels abroad (Berlin, Geneva, Paris, Florence, Rome, Venice, Milan, Genoa).

> Russo-Turkish War.

1878
Opera *Eugene Onegin* (after Pushkin). Concerto for violin and orchestra. Grand Sonata for piano. *Children's Album,* 24 piano pieces. Six
songs, opus 38. Liturgy of St. John Chrysostom. *Souvenir d'un lieu cher*
(*Méditation, Scherzo, Melodie*). Leaves Moscow Conservatory. Vaca-
tions at Nadezhda von Meck's estate.

232 Casimir Malevich is born. Failed assassination attempt by Vera Zasulich against St. Petersburg mayor Trepov. Chief of the gendarmerie Mezentsev is killed by terrorists.

1879
Opera *The Maid of Orleans* (after Schiller). Orchestral Suite no. 1. Travels abroad (Paris, Berlin, Rome).

Unsuccessful terrorist attack on Tsar Alexander II.

1880
Capriccio italien for orchestra. Piano Concerto no. 2. *Serenade* for string orchestra. *1812* Overture. Seven songs, opus 47. Father dies.

Dostoyevsky completes *The Brothers Karamazov.* Mikhail Fokine and Alexander Blok are born in St. Petersburg. Terrorists explode bomb in Winter Palace.

1881
Vespers for mixed choir a cappella. Travels abroad (Vienna, Florence, Venice, Rome, Naples, Nice, Paris).

Mussorgsky dies of alcoholism in St. Petersburg. Dostoyevsky dies. Anna Pavlova, Mikhail Larionov, Natalya Goncharova are born. Tsar Alexander II killed by a terrorist bomb; his heir, Alexander III, assumes the throne.

1882
Piano Trio "In Memory of a Great Artist" (Nikolai Rubinstein). Travels abroad (Sorrento, Florence, Berlin).

Premiere of Rimsky-Korsakov's opera *The Snow Maiden* at the Maryinsky Theater. Premiere of Glazunov's Symphony no. 1 and Quartet no. 1. A son, Igor, is born to Tchaikovsky's friend, Fyodor Stravinsky, basso of the Maryinsky Theater.

1883

Opera *Mazeppa* (after Pushkin). Orchestral Suite no. 2. Coronation March. Travels abroad (Paris, Berlin).

Turgenev dies in France.

1884

Orchestral Suite no. 3. Concerto Fantasy for piano and orchestra. Six songs, opus 57. First performance of *Eugene Onegin* at Maryinsky Theater. Travels abroad (Berlin, Paris, Davos, Zurich). Meets Glazunov.

Tolstoy's *Confession*. First collection of short stories by Anton Chekhov.

1885

Religious works for choir. *Manfred* Symphony (after Byron).

1886

Dumka for piano. Twelve songs, opus 60. Travels to Tiflis, then to the Mediterranean, Marseille, Paris. Meets Léo Delibes.

Tolstoy completes "The Death of Ivan Ilyich." Grand Duke Konstantin Romanov publishes his first book of verse.

234   **1887**

Opera *The Sorceress. Mozartiana.* "The Golden Cloud Slept" for chorus (poetry by Mikhail Lermontov). Six songs, opus 63, to words by Grand Duke Konstantin. Tchaikovsky begins regular conducting of his own works. A concert tour of Europe. Conducts at Gewandhaus, Leipzig. Meets Brahms and Grieg.

> First performance, composer conducting, of *Capriccio espagnol* by Rimsky-Korsakov. Marc Chagall born near Vitebsk.

1888

Symphony no. 5. *Hamlet* overture fantasy. Concert tour of Europe. In Berlin, meets Richard Strauss; in Leipzig, Gustav Mahler; in Prague, Antonín Dvořák.

> First performance, composer conducting, of *Schéhérazade* by Rimsky-Korsakov. Alexander Scriabin enters Moscow Conservatory. Chekhov's novella *The Steppe.*

1889

Ballet *The Sleeping Beauty.* Concert tour of Europe. Meets Chekhov, who promises to write a libretto based on Lermontov's *A Hero of Our Time.*

> Anna Akhmatova and Vaslav Nijinsky are born.

1890

Opera *The Queen of Spades* (after Pushkin). *Souvenir de Florence,* string sextet. Premiere of *The Sleeping Beauty* at the Maryinsky Theater (choreographed by Marius Petipa). Premiere of *The Queen of Spades* at Maryinsky Theater. Von Meck ceases monthly stipend. Correspondence with von Meck ends.

Mikhail Vrubel's painting *The Demon*. Boris
Pasternak is born.

1891
Opera *Iolanta*. Concert tour of America. Conducts at opening of Carnegie Hall.

Rachmaninoff arranges *The Sleeping Beauty* for piano four hands. Tolstoy's novella *Kreutzer Sonata*. Sergei Prokofiev is born.

1892
Ballet *The Nutcracker*. Premiere of *The Nutcracker* (choreographed by Lev Ivanov) and *Iolanta* at Maryinsky Theater. Trip to Europe. In Hamburg attends performance of *Eugene Onegin* conducted by Mahler. Attends fiftieth anniversary performance of Glinka's opera *Ruslan and Lyudmila* at Maryinsky Theater, where he is seen by the young Igor Stravinsky.

Scriabin publishes his Valse for piano, opus 1.

1893
Symphony no. 6 (*Pathétique*). Piano Concerto no. 3. Eighteen piano pieces, opus 72. Vocal duet *Romeo and Juliet* (completed by Sergei Taneyev). Attends premiere of Rachmaninoff's opera *Aleko*. Travels to Europe. Awarded honorary doctorate at Cambridge. Conducts premiere of *Pathétique* Symphony in St. Petersburg. Dies October 25 (November 6)—officially of cholera. Buried in St. Petersburg at St. Alexander Nevsky Monastery.

Rachmaninoff's Piano Trio "In Memory of a Great Artist" (Tchaikovsky). The Franco-Russian Alliance.

236 *George Balanchine* *(Georgy Melitonovich Balanchivadze)* *1904–1983*

1904

On January 9 (22) in St. Petersburg a son, Georgy, is born into the family of Georgian composer Meliton Balanchivadze.

Premiere of Chekhov's play *The Cherry Orchard* at the Moscow Art Theater. Alexander Blok's first collection of poetry, *Poems About the Beautiful Lady*. Natalya Goncharova's painting *Madonna*.

1913

Enters the St. Petersburg Imperial Theater School.

Diaghilev's "Russian Seasons" in Paris presents *Daphnis et Chloë* by Ravel (choreographed by Mikhail Fokine) and *Le Sacre du printemps* by Stravinsky (choreographed by Vaslav Nijinsky, sets and costumes by Roerich). Alexander Scriabin first performs his piano sonatas nos. 9 and 10. *Stone,* Osip Mandelstam's first collection of poetry, is published. Premiere of *Victory Over the Sun,* the futurist opera by Matyushin, Kruchenykh, and Malevich (subsidized by Zheverzheyev and Fokine's older brother, Alexander).

1917

Tsar Nicholas II is swept from the throne in Petrograd. Eight months later, power is seized by the Bolsheviks, led by Lenin.

1920

Enters the Petrograd Conservatory in the piano and composition class (to study there until 1923).

> Meyerhold presents the production of *Dawns* based on the play by Emile Verhaeren (designed by Vladimir Dmitriev). Civil war ends in Russia.

1921

Graduates from the Theater School and joins the ballet troupe of the Maryinsky Theater.

> Diaghilev stages *The Sleeping Beauty* in London; several numbers are orchestrated by Stravinsky. Anna Akhmatova's poetry collection *Plantain* and *Anno domini MCMXXI*. The poetry collection *Evenings Not Here* by Mikhail Kuzmin. The death in Petrograd of Alexander Blok. The New Economic Policy (NEP) is introduced in Russia.

1922

The first performances of Balanchine's Young Ballet.

> Kasyan Goleizovsky presents a program of experimental ballets by his Moscow studio. Fyodor Lopukhov becomes artistic director of the Maryinsky Theater Ballet. Premiere of Stravinsky's opera *Mavra*. Stanislavsky mounts an experimental staging of Tchaikovsky's *Eugene Onegin*.

1923

Performs in Fyodor Lopukhov's "Dance Symphony."

238   Dmitri Shostakovich graduates from the piano
class at the Petrograd Conservatory.

1924

Leaves Russia with Tamara Zheverzheyeva, Alexandra Danilova,
and Nikolai Efimov. Joins Diaghilev's company as Georges Balanchine.

Poulenc's *Les Biches* performed by Diaghilev's
Ballets Russes de Monte Carlo (choreographed
by Bronislava Nijinska). Rachmaninoff piano
recitals in London. Yevgeny Zamyatin's novel
We is published in England. Léon Bakst dies in
Paris. Lenin dies in Moscow.

1925

Choreographs premiere of Ravel's opera *L'Enfant et les sortiléges,* also a
new version of Stravinsky's *Le Chant du rossignol.*

1928

Choreographs Stravinsky's ballet *Apollon Musagète.*

Meliton Balanchivadze composes the Georgian National March. Glazunov leaves Russia.
Artist Georges Yakulov dies in Yerevan.

1929

Choreographs Prokofiev's ballet *Prodigal Son.*

Diaghilev dies in Venice. Mikhail Kuzmin's
last collection of poetry, *The Trout Breaks the
Ice,* published in Leningrad.

1933

Choreographs *Mozartiana* to Tchaikovsky's music. At Lincoln

Kirstein's invitation, moves to America.

> Russian émigré writer Ivan Bunin receives Nobel Prize. Hitler takes power in Germany. President Roosevelt establishes diplomatic relations with the Soviet Union.

1935
Official premiere of *Serenade* to Tchaikovsky's music.

> Fyodor Lopukhov choreographs Shostakovich's ballet *Bright Stream* for the Bolshoi Theater. Balanchine's younger brother, Andrei Balanchivadze, having graduated from the Leningrad Conservatory in 1931, accepts position teaching composition at the Tbilisi Conservatory. Casimir Malevich dies.

1937
Choreographs Stravinsky's *Le Baiser de la fée* and *Jeu de cartes* for the Stravinsky Festival at the Metropolitan Opera.

> In Georgia, Meliton Balanchivadze dies.

1940
On Balanchine's commission, Paul Hindemith writes *The Four Temperaments*.

> The Leningrad premiere of Prokofiev's *Romeo and Juliet*, choreographed by Mikhail Lavrovsky (with Galina Ulanova and Konstantin Sergeyev). Stravinsky's *Symphony in C.*

1941
Choreographs *Ballet Imperial* to Tchaikovsky's Piano Concerto no. 2.

240   Hitler attacks the Soviet Union.

1945
Choreographs the *pas de deux* from Tchaikovsky's *Sleeping Beauty*.

Hitler defeated.

1947
Theme and Variations to Tchaikovsky's Suite no. 3.

Nicholas Roerich dies.

1948
Choreographs premiere of Stravinsky's *Orpheus*, commissioned by Kirstein. First performances of the New York City Ballet.

> In the Soviet Union, Prokofiev, Shostakovich, and Khachaturian are condemned as formalist composers. In Moscow, artist Vladimir Dmitriev, one of the founders of the Young Ballet, dies.

1951
New York City Ballet presents the second act of *Swan Lake*.

1953
Choreographs *Valse Fantasie* by Glinka.

> Stalin and Prokofiev die on the same day. Andrei Balanchivadze becomes chairman of the Composer's Union of Georgia. Vladimir Tatlin dies.

1954

Choreographs Tchaikovsky's *Nutcracker.*

1956

Choreographs *Allegro Brillante* to Tchaikovsky's Piano Concerto no. 3.

1957

Choreographs Stravinsky's ballet *Agon;* composer dedicates it to Lincoln Kirstein and George Balanchine.

> Pavel Tchelitchev dies in Rome. Mstislav Dobujinsky dies in New York.

1958

Waltz-Scherzo to Tchaikovsky's music.

> Boris Pasternak refuses the Nobel Prize under pressure from the Soviet authorities.

1960

Pas de deux from Tchaikovsky's *Swan Lake.*

> Alexandre Benois dies in Paris.

1962–1963

New York City Ballet tours the Soviet Union. Balanchine returns to Moscow and Leningrad after 38 years; visits Georgia for the first time in his life; meets with his brother. Stages Tchaikovsky's *Eugene Onegin* in Hamburg. Choreographs *Movements for Piano and Orchestra* by Stravinsky and *Méditation* by Tchaikovsky.

> Stravinsky's triumphant visit to the Soviet Union, where the composer is received by

242   Premier Nikita Khrushchev. The Leningrad
Philharmonic under Yevgeny Mravinsky tours
the USA. Natalya Goncharova dies in Paris.

1969
Stages Glinka's opera *Ruslan and Lyudmila* in Hamburg.

1970
Choreographs Tchaikovsky's Suite no. 3.

        Kasyan Goleizovsky dies in Moscow.

1971
Stravinsky dies.

1972
Choreographs ballets to several major Stravinsky works for the
Stravinsky festival. New York City Ballet's second trip to Russia.

        Bronislava Nijinska dies in Los Angeles.

1975
Ravel festival at the New York City ballet.

        Dmitri Shostakovich dies in Moscow.

1981
Choreographs several works for the New York City Ballet Tchaikovsky Festival.

1982
New York City Ballet presents Stravinsky festival on the composer's
hundredth birthday.

1983

Awarded the Presidential Medal of Freedom, the highest civilian honor in the United States. On April 30, dies in New York.

PICTURE CREDITS

INDEX

Adagio Lamentoso (ballet), 21

After Babel (Steiner), 15

Agon (ballet), 217

Akhmatova, Anna, 20, 65

Alexander II, Tsar, 44

Alexander III, Tsar, 44, 45, 60, 161

Alexandra Feodorovna, Tsarina, 60

Alexandrinsky Imperial Theater, St. Petersburg, 52, 65, 164, 196

Ali, Muhammad, 152

Andersen, Hans Christian, 205

Andersen, Ib, 128

Andrianov, Samuel Konstantinovich, 63–64, 157

Apollo (ballet), 205, 217

Apollon Musagète (Stravinsky), 217

Argutinsky, Prince, 57, 80

L'Arlésienne (ballet), 113

Auer, Leopold, 167

Ave Verum (Mozart), 127

Le Baiser de la fée (ballet), 205, 217

Balanchivadze, Andrei, 112

Balanchivadze, Meliton Antonovich, 111–12

Ballets Russes, 21, 215

Barzin, Leon, 197

Beethoven, Ludwig van, 32–33, 96, 162, 189

Bellini, Vincenzo, 40

Benois, Alexandre, 57, 178–79, 215

Bizet, Georges, 113

La Bohème (Puccini), 99

246 Bolshoi Ballet, 198
Bolshoi Theater, 157, 158
Boris Godunov (Mussorgsky), 112
Bortnyansky, Dmitri, 130
Botticelli, Sandro, 211–12
Buffon, Comte Georges-Louis
Leclerc de, 43
Busch, Wilhelm, 44

Conservatory, St. Petersburg,
57, 64, 75
Cooper, James Fenimore, 107
Le Coq d'Or (Rimsky-Korsakov),
196
Coronation Cantata (Tchai-
kovsky), 45
Craft, Robert, 206
Croce, Arlene, 19

Cabinet of Dr. Caligari, The
(film), 154
Caesar and Cleopatra (Shaw), 196
Canticum sacrum (Stravinsky),
130
Capriccio italien (ballet), 34
Carmen (Bizet), 113
Carnegie Hall, New York City,
105
Chanel, Coco, 85
Le chant du rossignol (ballet), 166
Chateaubriand, Vicomte
Francois-Auguste-René de,
43
Chekhov, Mikhail, 96, 107, 146
Chekrygin, Alexander, 168
Cherevichki (Tchaikovsky), 205
Children's Album (Tchaikovsky),
205
Chinizelli's Circus, St. Peters-
burg, 69
Chopin, Frederic, 115
Church of Christ the Saviour,
St. Petersburg, 46, 93
Clock Symphony (Haydn), 119
Concert Fantasy (ballet), 34
Conservatory, Moscow, 64, 79,
83

d'Amboise, Jacques, 34
"Dance Symphony" (*The Gran-
deur of the Universe*) (ballet),
69, 70, 162, 164, 166–67,
189
Danilova, Alexandra (Shura),
69, 98, 146, 167, 206
Daphnis et Chloë (ballet), 203
Davidsbündlertänze (ballet), 21
Davydov, Vladimir (Bob), 98
"Death of Ivan Ilyich, The"
(Tolstoy), 96
Demon (Lermontov), 222
Derain, André, 212
Diaghilev, Sergei, 21, 33, 44, 57,
82, 85, 102, 152, 166, 178,
179, 207–8, 210–12, 213
Dmitriev, Vladimir (Volodya),
164, 165, 166, 214–15
Don Giovanni (Mozart), 40
Donizetti, Gaetano, 40
Dostoyevsky, Fyodor, 92, 96
Drigo, Riccardo (Richard Ev-
genievich), 56–57, 126, 146
Drum Roll Symphony (Haydn),
119
Dumas, Alexandre *père*, 43, 176,
178

Duncan, Isadora, 162, 214

Edgeworth, Miss, 43
Education Maternelle (Tastu), 43
Efimov, Nikolai, 69, 98, 146
L'Enfant et les sortilèges (Ravel), 34, 203
Erbstein, Boris, 166
Ernst, Max, 212
Eroica. See Third Symphony (Beethoven)
Esmeralda (ballet), 155–56
Eugene Onegin (Tchaikovsky), 31, 45, 52, 133–40, 188

Fairbanks, Douglas, 107
Fairy Doll, The (ballet), 126
Family Education (Edgeworth), 43
Famous Children (Mason), 43
Farrell, Suzanne, 128, 150
Feuillet d'album (Tchaikovsky), 205
Féval, Paul, 43
Fifth Symphony (Tchaikovsky), 33, 77, 118, 119, 122
Firebird (Stravinsky), 123, 217
First Piano Concerto (Tchaikovsky), 33, 34, 79
First Symphony (Tchaikovsky), 118, 205
Foa, Eugenie, 43
Fokine, Mikhail, 154, 162, 164, 177, 212–13
Formalism, 160
Fortress of Peter and Paul, St. Petersburg, 55, 59

Four Temperaments, The (ballet), 247
197–98
Fourth Symphony (Beethoven), 162
Fourth Symphony (Tchaikovsky), 119, 123
Fox-trot, 70–71

Garbuzova, Raya, 197
Gavlikovsky, Nikolai Ludvigovich, 64
Le Génie du Christianisme (Chateaubriand), 43
Gerdt, Pavel, 56
Geva, Tamara. See Zheverzheyeva, Tamara
Glazunov, Alexander Konstantinovich, 57, 77, 165
Glière, Reinhold, 160–61
Glinka, Mikhail, 15, 44, 108–11, 146, 221
Gluck, Christoph Willibald von, 164
Goethe, Johann Wolfgang von, 96
Gogol, Nikolai, 215
Goldwyn, Sam, 154
Goleizovsky, Kasyan, 81, 113, 149
Goncharov, Ivan, 79
Gounod, Charles, 205
Griboyedov, Alexander, 63
Grin, Alexander, 189
Grossvatertanz, 179

Hamlet (Tchaikovsky), 127
Hanslick, Eduard, 131

248

Harlequinade (ballet), 57, 154
Hart, William, 107
Haydn, Franz Joseph, 117, 119
Headless Horseman (Reid), 107
Heifetz, Yascha, 167
Hero of Our Time, A (Lermontov), 222–23
Hindemith, Paul, 197
Hoffmann, E. T. A., 66, 96, 175, 177–78, 184–85, 189, 190
Horgan, Barbara, 18, 23

Imperial St. Petersburg Theatrical School. *See* Maryinsky Theater
Iolanta (Tchaikovsky), 78, 140
Irving, Robert, 118
Ivanov, Lev, 146, 154, 158, 159, 175, 176
Ivanova, Lida, 98, 146–47, 148
Ivan Susanin. See Life for the Tsar, A (Glinka)

Jacolio, Louis, 43
Jeu de cartes (ballet), 90, 127

Kachalov, Vassili, 146
Keynes, John Maynard, 163
Khovanshchina (Mussorgsky), 216
Kirstein, Lincoln, 106, 156
Kistler, Darci, 152
Kochno, Boris, 210, 211–12
Konstantin Romanov, Grand Duke, 69, 73–74, 135, 199
Kopeikin, Nikolai, 58, 197

Korovin, Konstantin, 169
Kostelanetz, Andre, 196
Krauss, Werner, 70
Kresty prison, St. Petersburg, 112
Kuzmin, Mikhail, 65–66

Laroche, Hermann, 78, 122, 123, 144, 147, 153, 158, 164, 165, 177, 184, 190, 221
Last of the Mohicans (Cooper), 107
Leningrad Philharmonic, 122
Lermontov, Mikhail, 95, 96, 97, 126
Life for the Tsar, A (Glinka), 44, 109, 111
Linder, Max, 154
Liszt, Franz, 162
Litrov, Nazar, 138
Little Humpbacked Horse, The (ballet), 60, 61, 146, 160
Lopukhov, Fyodor, 21, 69, 70, 161–64, 166–67, 168, 189, 215
Lourié, Arthur, 206
"Love of a Dead Man" (Lermontov), 222
Lucrezia (Donizetti), 102
Ludus Tonalis (Hindemith), 198
Lunacharsky, Anatoly, 68

Magic Flute, The (ballet), 146, 154, 159
Magic Flute, The (Mozart), 112
Maid of Orleans, The (Tchai-

kovsky), 204

Makarova, Natalia (Natasha), 212

Mardzhanov, Konstantin, 141

Martins, Peter, 34

Maryinsky Theater, St. Petersburg, 20, 56, 59–70, 111, 144, 153, 161, 164, 165, 167, 168, 169, 213, 215

Mason, Michel, 43

"Matelot" (ballet), 69

Matisse, Henri, 212

Mavra (Stravinsky), 109, 206

Max und Moritz (Busch), 44

Mazeppa (Tchaikovsky), 52, 140, 204

Meditation (Tchaikovsky), 131

Memoirs of the Devil (Soulier), 43

Merkling, Anna, 220

Meyerhold, Vsevolod, 57, 164, 166

Midsummer Night's Dream, A (Shakespeare), 127

Mikhailovsky Theater, St. Petersburg, 196

Milstein, Nathan, 167, 197

Milyukova, Antonina, 83–84

Mimika, 154

Minkus, Ludwig (Léon), 198–99

Moscow Art Theater, 146

Mozart, Wolfgang Amadeus, 40, 109–10, 112, 127, 200–201

Mozartiana (ballet), 19, 34, 127, 128

Mravinsky, Evgeny, 121–22

Mungalova, Olga (Olya), 69

Murzilki, 43

Mussorgsky, Modest, 112, 216

Mysterious Island, The (Verne), 42

Napravnik, Eduard, 185

Nevada Meat Market, New York City, 11

Nevsky Prospect, St. Petersburg, 54

New Yorker, The, 19

Nicholas II, Tsar, 60, 67

Nichols, Kyra, 150

Nightingale, The (Stravinsky), 165–66

Nijinska, Bronislava, 214

Nijinsky, Vaslav, 213–14

Nikolai, Father, 101

Nikolsky Cathedral, St. Petersburg, 48

Les Noces (ballet), 123, 214

Nutcracker, The (ballet), 56, 67, 175–93

Oblomov (Goncharov), 79

Oblomovism, 78–79

Octet for Wind Instruments (Stravinsky), 206

Opera de Monte Carlo, 203

Orfeo ed Euridice (Gluck), 164

Orpheus (ballet), 156, 217

Pantomime, 153–54

Le Pas d'Acier (ballet), 166

Pathétique. See Sixth Symphony (Tchaikovsky)

Pavlova, Anna, 213

249

250 People's House, St. Petersburg,
       196
     Perrault, Charles, 161
     Perséphone (Stravinsky), 123
     Peterburgskaya gazeta, 159
     Peterburgskii listok, 204
     Peter the Great, Tsar, 51, 52
     Petipa, Marius, 22, 28, 29, 57,
       61, 155, 158, 161, 167,
       168–70, 175, 176, 178, 188,
       191, 198–99, 212, 214
     Les Petits Musiciens (Foa), 43
     Petrouchka (ballet), 123, 179, 217
     Polovetsian Dances (Borodin),
       196
     Poor Eugen (*Hinkemann*) (Toller),
       65, 164
     Préludes (Liszt), 162
     La Primavera (Botticelli), 211–12
     Prodigal Son (ballet), 210–11
     Prokofiev, Sergei, 21, 35, 166,
       209, 210–11
     Pulcinella (ballet), 214–15
     Pushkin, Alexander, 15, 52, 95,
       96, 133, 134–35, 138, 170,
       222

     Queen of Spades, The (Pushkin),
       133, 178, 179
     Queen of Spades, The (Tchai-
       kovsky), 31, 52, 90, 118,
       133–41, 179, 205, 222

     Rachmaninoff, Sergei, 21,
       206–9, 211
     Radlov, Sergei, 65, 196
     "Ratcatcher, The" (Grin), 189

     Ravel, Maurice, 34, 203, 216
     Raymonda (ballet), 57
     Reid, Mayne, 107
     Requiem (Stravinsky), 130
     Rimsky-Korsakov, Nikolai, 78,
       111, 123, 127, 162, 196, 216
     Robbins, Jerome, 34
     Romanov, Boris (Bobisha), 81,
       113
     Romeo and Juliet (Tchaikovsky),
       127
     Roosevelt Hospital, New York
       City, 22
     Rossini, Gioacchino, 40
     Rostropovich, Mstislav, 35
     Rouault, Georges, 212
     Rubinstein, Anton, 78
     Rubinstein, Arthur, 150
     Rubinstein, Nikolai, 79, 81, 144
     Ruslan and Lyudmila (Glinka), 44,
       111
     Russian roulette, 21, 222–23

     Le Sacre du printemps (Stra-
       vinsky), 217
     St. Catherine's Day, 45–46
     Saint-Saëns, Camille, 143–44,
       197
     St. Vladimir's church, St. Pe-
       tersburg, 47, 181
     Salome (Wilde), 141
     Samson et Dalila (ballet), 197
     Savoyarov, Mikhail, 161
     Schéhérazade (Rimsky-Korsakov),
       162
     Schiller, Johann Christoph
       Friedrich von, 96–97

School of Jurisprudence, St. Petersburg, 41–42
Schopenhauer, Arthur, 96
Schumann, Robert, 113, 115
Scriabin, Alexander, 209–10
Second Piano Concerto (Tchaikovsky), 129–30
Second Suite (Tchaikovsky), 126
Second Symphony (Tchaikovsky), 118–19, 123
Serenade (ballet), 33, 35, 128–29, 214
Sergeyev, Nikolai, 167
Sevigne, Mme. de, 43
Shakespeare, William, 127
Shaw, George Bernard, 196
Shostakovich, Dmitri, 20
Shot, The (Pushkin), 222
Sibelius, Jean, 146
Sixth Symphony (*Pathétique*) (Tchaikovsky), 21, 119–22, 123, 195, 214, 219–20, 225
Sleeping Beauty, The (ballet), 31, 33, 56, 69, 143, 146, 159, 161, 167–69, 188, 205, 215
Slonimsky, Yuri, 166
Smirnova, Elena, 113
Sobeshchanskaya, Anna, 198–99
Sobinov, Leonid, 137
La Société des auteurs et compositeurs dramatiques, 210–11
Sollertinsky, Ivan, 166–67, 189, 190
Sorceress, The (Tchaikovsky), 140, 204
Soulier, Frederic, 43

Souvenir de Florence (ballet), 34
Spinoza, Benedict de, 96
Steiner, George, 15
Stravinsky, Fyodor (Fedya), 101, 204
Stravinsky, Igor Fyodorovich, 15, 22, 44, 52, 68, 89, 92, 100–101, 102, 123, 130, 139, 153, 156, 165–66, 179, 188, 198, 202–6, 211, 213, 214, 216–17
Stravinsky, Soulima (Svetik), 101
Struwelpeter (Hoffmann), 43
Styopka-Rastryopka, 43
Sue, Eugène, 43
Swan Lake (ballet), 64, 143, 146, 153, 156–60, 214

Taras, John, 34
Tastu, Amable, 43
Tchaikovsky, Anatoly, 84
Tchaikovsky, Modest, 65, 122, 143–44
Tchelitchev, Pavel (Pavlik), 212
Telemann, Georg Philipp, 34
Telyakovsky, Vladimir, 213
Tempest, The (Tchaikovsky), 127
Theater of Academic Drama. *See* Alexandrinsky Imperial Theater
Third Piano Concerto (Tchaikovsky), 130
Third Suite (Tchaikovsky), 126
Third Symphony (*Eroica*) (Beethoven), 189
Third Symphony (Tchaikovsky), 118–19

252 Toller, Ernst, 65, 196
Tolstoy, Leo, 92, 96
Turgenev, Ivan, 96
Twenty Thousand Leagues Under the Sea (Verne), 42

UFA Studio, 70
Uffizi Gallery, Florence, 211
Undine (Tchaikovsky), 157
Uspensky Cathedral, 46
Utrillo, Maurice, 212

La Valse (Ravel), 203
Valse Fantasie (ballet), 111
Valses nobles et sentimentales (Ravel), 203
Valse Triste (ballet), 146
Variations on a Theme by Corelli (Rachmaninoff), 208–9
Vedel, Artemi, 130
Veidt, Conrad, 70
Verne, Jules, 42

Vespers (Tchaikovsky), 130
Violin Concerto (Tchaikovsky), 131
Volynsky, Akim, 145, 163–64
von Meck, Nadezhda, 64, 76, 83, 85–86, 130, 131, 196
Vsevolozhsky, Ivan, 161

War and Peace (Prokofiev), 35
Wilde, Oscar, 141, 221
Winter Palace, St. Petersburg, 52

Yakulov, Georges, 166
Young Ballet, 69, 149, 167

Zajaczkowsky, Henry, 12n
Zheverzheyev, Levky Ivanovich, 57–59
Zheverzheyeva, Tamara, 57, 59, 84, 98, 146
Zoo, St. Petersburg, 59

ABOUT THE AUTHOR

Solomon Volkov was born in 1944 in the USSR and received his diploma with honors from the Leningrad Conservatory, where he continued graduate work in musicology until 1971. In 1971 his book *Young Composers of Leningrad* appeared with a preface by Dmitri Shostakovich, and Mr. Volkov became a senior editor of *Sovetskaya Muzyka*, the journal of the USSR Ministry of Culture and the Union of Cómposers. He came to the United States in 1976 and, in 1979, published *Testimony: The Memoirs of Dmitri Shostakovich*, which was written by him in collaboration with the composer, while in the USSR. *Testimony* received the 1980 ASCAP-Deems Taylor Award for excellence in writing about music. Called by the London *Times* "the book of the year," *Testimony* has been translated into twelve major languages, and has been published in seventeen editions. Now an American citizen, Mr. Volkov lives as a freelance author in New York with his wife, Marianna Volkov, a pianist and photographer.